Blues
Mandolin
Man

Blues Mandolin Man

The Life and Music of Yank Rachell

Richard Congress

University Press of Mississippi
Jackson

American Made Music Series
Advisory Board

David Evans, General Editor
Barry Jean Ancelet
Edward A. Berlin
Joyce J. Bolden
Rob Bowman
Susan C. Cook
Curtis Ellison
William Ferris
Michael Harris
John Edward Hasse
Kip Lornell
Frank McArthur
W. K. McNeil
Bill Malone
Eddie S. Meadows
Manuel H. Peña
Wayne D. Shirley
Robert Walser
Charles Wolfe

www.upress.state.ms.us

Copyright © 2001 by University Press of Mississippi
All rights reserved

09 08 07 06 05 04 03 02 01   4 3 2 1
∞

Photo on page ii by Patrick Schneider, courtesy of the *Indianapolis Star*.

Library of Congress Cataloging-in-Publication Data
Congress, Richard.
Blues mandolin man : the life and music of Yank Rachell / Richard Congress.
p. cm. — (American made music series)
Includes bibliographical references (p.   ), discography (p.   ), and index.
ISBN 1-57806-333-7 (cloth : alk. paper) — ISBN 1-57806-334-5 (pbk. : alk. paper)
1. Rachell, Yank.   2. Blues musicians—United States—Biography.
3. Afro-American musicians—Biography.   4. Blues (Music)—History and criticism.   I. Title.   II. Series.
ML419.R36 C66 2001
781.643'092—dc21
[B]
00-047729

British Library Cataloging-in-Publication Data available

To Helen

Contents

Foreword ix
Acknowledgments xiii
Introduction xv

Blues Mandolin Man 3

Appendix 1
Comments on Yank Rachell's Mandolin Style 89
Rich DelGrosso

Appendix 2
Comments on Yank Rachell's Guitar Style 93
David Evans

Appendix 3
Interviews 97

Appendix 4
Musicians 125

Appendix 5
Brownsville Lynching 139

Discography 143
Selected Song Lyrics 159
Bibliography 177
Index 179

Foreword

The decade of the 1990s saw a severe diminution of the ranks of blues singers and musicians who had been active in the years before World War II. In fact, only a handful are now left as we enter the twenty-first century. While many interviews of early blues artists have been published over the years, only a few of these figures were fortunate to be able to tell their own stories in a book-length format. This usually required that the person be someone of significance in blues history, someone of great achievement as a singer, instrumentalist, songwriter, or interpreter, usually someone with a major recording career who influenced the music's stylistic development and interacted with other important musical figures.

There can be little doubt about the importance of James "Yank" Rachell in the history of the blues. He is one of only two major blues mandolinists and the only one to carry that instrument to any degree into the blues revival scene from the 1960s onward. The mandolin is not a soloist's instrument, and its player therefore requires one or more musical partners. Rachell's story is rich in musical associations, and it reveals for the first time at some length the workings of the blues scene in West Tennessee outside the city of Memphis. This was a scene that produced such important figures as Sleepy John Estes and John Lee "Sonny Boy" Williamson. Rachell performed and recorded with these and other artists from a region that was every bit as important as the nearby Mississippi Delta in the development of blues styles. Many of the root forms of modern blues ensembles can be found in the kinds of groups that Rachell played in during the 1920s, 1930s, and 1940s in West Tennessee. The region's blues were especially characterized by fine song writing and the sharing of lyrical and musical ideas. Themes that Yank Rachell recorded also turn up in the blues of Estes, Williamson, and other artists from the area, and it would be difficult to determine which artist actually created any particular theme. Among the songs that Rachell shared with others in the region were "Sugar Farm Blues," "Stack o' Dollars Blues," "Gravel Road Woman," "Up North Blues," and "Tappin' That Thing." Other compositions of his, such as "Lake Michigan Blues," "Hobo Blues," ".38 Pistol Blues," "Biscuit-Bakin' Woman," "Yellow Yam Blues," and "Peach Tree Blues," have gone on to become standards in the blues repertoire and be performed by artists who may be unaware that they were originally recorded by Yank Rachell.

The subject of any book-length autobiography should also be a raconteur able to tell a story rich in detail about both a life and a way of life in an environment of art and entertainment, mingled with family relationships, work outside of music, travel, friendships, love, loss, and the sweep of passing events both local and national. Rachell succeeds in this respect, revealing a warm storytelling style with a concern for truth and accuracy when it comes to musical information but an ability to embellish and dramatize more personal anecdotes.

Finally, since most people involved in blues music in the early years came from backgrounds in which formal education was scarcely available or little stressed, the subject of an autobiography normally needs a sympathetic and knowledgeable collaborator/editor, who can help extract the story, arrange it in a logical fashion, and place it in a context of other known facts about the subject and his or her environment. Fortunately, Yank Rachell found his collaborator in Richard Congress, one of a number of blues researchers and enthusiasts in the 1990s who realized how precious were the memories of the few remaining major early blues artists, one who had the foresight and diligence to help one such artist tell his story.

David Evans
The University of Memphis
February 2000

Acknowledgments

I would like to thank the people who helped me in this project.

To my lifelong friend Craig Pinkus, thanks for giving me the idea to write this book. To Matt Watson of the Smithsonian Jazz Oral History Project, Ed Komara, director of the University of Mississippi Blues Archive, Jay Zochowski of radio station WFYI, and blues researcher Gayle Wardlow, I express my appreciation for pointing me in the right direction for my research. Thanks to *Living Blues* magazine for supplying me with back issues (including the March/April 1988 issue, which featured an interview with Yank Rachell). Thanks to Brenda Sellari of the Heywood County Chamber of Commerce for her suggestions for research and historical information. Thanks to musicians Beki Brindle and Larry DeMyer for introducing me to Yank, facilitating my interviews, and helping me contact other sources of information. I'm grateful to Yank's daughter Maenell and granddaughter Sheena for their hospitality and cooperation. Also, thanks to George Fish for his help in locating people to interview. To musicians Pat Webb, Allen Stratyner, Dave Morgan, Peter Roller, Ry Cooder, Charlie Musselwhite, Andra Fay McIntire, and

Rich DelGrosso, many thanks for sharing their experiences playing the blues with Yank. And again thanks to Rich DelGrosso for his knowledge about jug band music, the mandolin, and Yank's way of playing. To Robert Koester of Delmark Records, thanks for giving me background information on Yank and Sleepy John Estes and their recordings. To Doris Johnson of the Indiana Blues Society and Hal Yeagey, owner of the Slippery Noodle, thanks for sharing their experiences. And a heartfelt thanks to Yank's friends and contemporaries, bluesmen John Brim, Henry Townsend, Dave "Honeyboy" Edwards, and Howard "Louie Bluie" Armstrong, for taking the time to talk with me.

I also want to thank Hettie Jones for teaching me about writing, editing, and persistence and thank Margaret Wolf and Richard Valcourt for helping me improve this work.

Chris Smith performed the important and arduous task of checking the discography for accuracy, and Kip Lornell did similar service by looking up the copyright status of quoted song lyrics. Many thanks to both of them.

Thanks also to my editor David Evans for keeping me on the straight and narrow and not allowing me to let things slide. (I'm not a natural born researcher; it's too much hard work!)

And, finally, thanks to my wife, Helen Schiff, who encouraged and supported me in this endeavor with a minimum of teasing.

Introduction

On April 9, 1997, eighty-seven-year-old blues mandolin man James "Yank" Rachell died at home in his sleep. Three hundred people filled the pews at the Nazarene Missionary Baptist Church for his funeral in Indianapolis on April 19. Regular church parishioners and Yank's large family occupied about half of the church's sanctuary. The other half was taken up by blues musicians and fans, young and old, black and white. From Chicago, John Brim, seventy-five, Dave "Honeyboy" Edwards, eighty-two, and Jimmy Walker, ninety-two, came to send off their old friend and fellow bluesman. Yank's mandolin was on display next to his casket, and among the flowers was an arrangement sent by B. B. King, who had once told Yank, "It's people like you who made people like me possible." Music for the funeral service was provided by the Mighty Quotations, a gospel quartet formed by Yank's son, J. C. Rachell, who had died of diabetes in 1996.

Born March 16, 1910, into a world powered by mules and illuminated by coal-oil lanterns, Yank grew up the son of sharecroppers on a farm outside of the West Tennessee town of Brownsville. But his musical talent and lifelong friendship with Sleepy John Estes enabled him to lead a different sort of life from that of the usual exploited southern black laborer. The two of them were playing in a jug band on the streets of Memphis in 1929 when a talent scout for Victor Records came looking for southern "race" music to record. The recordings they made then opened up different horizons for the nineteen-year-old Yank.

By the time of his death, just about everyone else of Yank's musical generation was long gone. It would have been hard to find many blues musicians still living and still musically active—which Yank was, up to the day he died—who started recording in 1929. B. B. King, whose popularity reaches far beyond a strictly blues audience, is seventy-five and first recorded in 1949. John Lee Hooker, another well-known and heavily recorded bluesman, whose style has greatly influenced rock and roll, is eighty-three and began recording in 1948.

Jay Zochowski, who hosts the blues program "Nothing but the Blues" on public radio station WFYI in Indianapolis, described Yank Rachell as "a window on the past. His playing sheds light on what was going on musically back in the 1920s and how it shaped the blues we have today."

I grew up in Indianapolis and heard Yank play at a coffeehouse when I was still living there in 1966. Like many other blues musicians who had recorded before World War II and then dropped out of sight, Yank had been "rediscovered" with the folk music revival of the 1960s.

Thirty years later, in a casual telephone conversation with a longtime friend who is a lawyer in Indianapolis, I again heard about Yank Rachell. My friend told me he was trying to help Yank recover any royalty money that might be due him. It was news to me that Yank was still alive, so it didn't take long for me to decide to head back to my hometown to talk with Yank. As a blues and jazz enthusiast I believe that the experiences and memories of blues musicians of his generation are well worth preserving and passing on. Although Yank was no superstar, he was a unique stylist, stubbornly staying with the mandolin, which most people see as an odd or old-fashioned instrument, and he led a long life immersed in the blues.

In July of 1996 I traveled to Indianapolis from New York to tape interviews with Yank. In November and then February of the following year, I returned to tape more sessions. On April 9 Larry DeMyer, an Indianapolis musician and close friend of Yank, telephoned to tell me that Yank had died.

In the course of our conversation DeMyer said, "Well, the saga is over," and a saga it truly was. His life spanned and reflected much of the history of the blues and a lot of social history and struggle.

My discussions with Yank were cut short by his death, and this would have been a better work if I had been able to spend more time talking with him. I did have the advantage and pleasure of interviewing many people: musicians, blues writers, record producers, and musicologists who worked with or knew Yank. I was struck by the uniformity of their evaluation of the man. The words "steady," "reliable," and "kind hearted" came up most frequently. Blues harmonica star Charlie Musselwhite spoke fondly of how Yank took him under his wing and showed him the ropes when he was an eighteen-year-old novice. Many musicians were also influenced by Yank's style of music. It was from listening to Yank's recordings with Sleepy John Estes that the innovative musician and composer Ry Cooder learned to play blues on the mandolin.

The narrative core of this book is based on my transcriptions and editing of taped interviews with Yank. Despite the short time I spent with him, I think I succeeded in capturing a large enough slice of his long life, as he related it to me in his down-to-earth language, with his humor and infectious laugh, to give readers a living picture of this man, the blues mandolin man, Yank Rachell.

Blues Mandolin Man

Chapter 1

Well, in the house when I was growin' up we had them old straw ticks, you know, made out of straw, bed tick. Straw in 'em. And then you have them shucks tore up and put in your bed. Well, you sleep on that. Didn't have no mattress or nothin' like that then. Way back, didn't have no mattress. No.

You work all day, go out in the fields and work from sun to sun. Come back, you take a bath in an old tin tub and wash. But you got to pack the water, carry it in a pail, you know, and make a fire and heat the water before you get in the tub to take a bath. Had that old, big bar of yellow soap and you take a bath in that. And you go to bed and get up in the morning. You go to the field about sunup, and the sun go down and you come back in and you got to pack that water again. Make a fire and heat up the water and take a bath.

My family sharecropped. The man furnish you a house and furnish you with a team of horses to work with. And the man go to town and open up a trade for you, so you'd get your groceries. And about every week you'd go and get groceries or something, get an allowance, to carry you that week. My daddy didn't own no tools. The man furnish everything. Furnish your mules, plow, and tools. At the end of the year you had to pay what he furnish you, groceries, coffee, flour. That fall when you get your cotton you had to pay him.

The end of the year come the man say, "Well, you like to got out this year, but next year maybe you'll pay out." See, they done got all the money then, you know. There wadn't nothin' for you. "But maybe you'll get out and git it up next year. You lack a little payin' it all out. Next year maybe you'll make it out." You clear some money in a way. But you'll never clear out, never get out of debt.

"Well, maybe you'll get out next year." They done got all the money. All that kind of stuff, you know. He say that. He out there settin' under a tree. He out settin' on the porch and you, you're out there in the hot sun, hoeing cotton row by row.

My daddy used to cook sorghum, make molasses and everything. Sorghum grow like corn, and you go out and cut that sorghum and you cut the head off, lay it down there. And they got a mill. You hitch your mule to it and you take that sorghum and you put it in that mill. And that mill go around and ground that juice out the sorghum. It run into that pan. They got a long pan to cook it in and they skim it. And the mule goin' around and around.

The sorghum get done, then they put it in jars. And they make that good molasses. They keep it too long, it turn to sugar. In wintertime you don't feel like cookin'. You put bread in the fireplace and rake back the ashes. Make up some cornbread and put it down in there in those bricks. Put some ashes over the top of the bread. It come out brown. It ash cake. Brush it off and eat it with that sorghum that went to sugar, you got a good dish. Eat some side meat. You done kill a hog, and you eat that. We enjoyed it.

I was seven years old when I started to work in the fields, until I was about seventeen. Seventeen, eighteen, I hung it up! I hung it up, man. Gettin' that old mule and hitch 'em up. Plow one row at a time. Ohhhhhhhh!

Twelve o'clock bell ring and you go to the house, eat lunch. Then you go back out there. Well, you may go out early in the morning. Come out about eleven o'clock. It's hot. Wait until later in the evening and go back when it's cool. You lay back your cotton, and later, after a while, you see your cotton blooming. After while, cotton boll come on. Later on cotton open and then you gonna get them old long sacks, start pickin' cotton.

Got a big wagon and you empty that cotton in there and take it to a gin. They take the lint off that cotton and leave the seed. Well, we get the seed on it, some of it. And they make a bale of cotton out of it. They got things to make a big bale of cotton. Five hundred pounds, that what they do all day long. Five hundred dollar for a bale of cotton. You may raise five bale of cotton, you may have ten bale of cotton.

The man go round with a sample.

"Well, we goin' see how much cotton is today." And he carry the sample up there. Come back.

"Well, they say so much a pound. You want to sell your bale?"

"Yeah."

Take the bale up there and sell it. Get some money out of it. And he get the money. You done got the seed money and you gin your cotton. The seed come out of the cotton. But the lint, they bale it up.

I'm telling you, man, country's something else. But I enjoyed it. I didn't know no better. I lived so far back in the country my breath smelled like cordwood!

We was livin' on the man's farm. He own that house, the man furnish you a house to stay in. We grow cotton, corn, peas, all of that. But the main thing is the cotton. That's what made the money. Other things you use.

Some peoples get so far in debt they run off the land. Some of 'em did that, run off. 'Cause they got too much in debt. No. We stayed there. Worked for the white people. Bailin' hay, plowin', cuttin' wood. I never did run off. Always tried to do the right thing. I ain't got no background that I know of, from my days up to now. They got nothin' about Yank. Now some of 'em rent. When you rent a place, everything on the farm is yours. Say you rent twenty acres, well, everything you raise on it is yours.

My daddy didn't like the city. I tried to get him to come to the city. No, he ain't comin' up here eatin' wasp's nests. He called white bread wasp's nests. He said, "I ain't eatin' that wasp's nest. I want to eat me some corn bread and stay on the farm and raise my meat." And that's what he did. He never did come into the city. After I growed up, I left and stayed in the city. But I go out and see about 'em and sometime make a crop with 'em, but I'll be in the city.

My daddy was Indian, part Indian. He used to carry mail on a horse and buggy. Ya got ya a mailbox, ya hear him: "Hayoooooo!" Hand raised. He use to carry mail and he always talk about north. Go north. Don't stay here amongst these folks. Go north. Had Indian in him. Don't know what tribe.

'Round our house nothing but trees, grass, out in the country. In the old country house you could lay in bed and see the sun rise. Them old cracks in the house. My house was about half a mile from the road. It was made of wood. Some of 'em were made of logs and had that dirt between the logs. We had shutters, no glass windows. They didn't paint no house then, not in the country. Inside the house we didn't have much furniture. Some of the houses I lived in — we moved around some and work on another farm — had a porch, some didn't.

Had a barn there, chickens and a henhouse. Daddy had a vegetable garden. Had greens, onions, sweet potatoes, white potatoes, peas. Didn't have to buy nothing much but a little flour and a little sugar and coffee. We raised everything. Ain't like here, you have to pay for water and sewer and all that junk.

When I got big enough to work, I could haul cotton, corn. Had to walk a piece to the field. Take that long hoe, and hoe that cotton.

I had two brothers. They worked in the fields too. Leslie was the oldest brother. A. B. was the baby boy. I'm the middle son. We all used to play music together, we three brothers.

They passed away a long time ago. The baby boy, he was seventeen when he passed away. My baby brother was on a wagon one day. They had to haul wood. Went out in the country to cut wood in the bottoms, in the woods. So we could make a fire or something. So he was in the wagon up there and his foot slipped under the wagon and knocked the leg out of whack. Got his knee joint out of whack. So he went home. My daddy tried to put his leg back in shape, but that leg was infected and that killed him.

When my older brother passed he was 'bout twenty. Leslie worked for a man had a peach orchard. He was spraying that peach orchard and that spray killed him. A man sell them peaches; he had a big orchard, Robert Doolin. He work there for the man four or five years, but sprayin' them trees with that poison got him. And that left me with nobody. Then me and Sleepy John run up together.

My brother Leslie made moonshine. He'd cook it out in the wood and we'd drink that stuff. Sometime we'd drink it as it came out of the little thing before it went in bottles. We didn't care. The mash, you know. Sleepy John made a song about it: "... been drinkin' moonshine, harm many a man." Sonny Boy did too, both of 'em made that song.[1]

Both my parents work. My mother worked until eleven o'clock, she come home and fix dinner. 'Bout twelve we go and eat. Then one o'clock we all go back to the fields. At night when we all come back she cook supper. We eat supper, then go to bed. 'Fore that we go and pack that water, take a bath, and go to bed. Next morning we get up we hear the old man out there sharpening that hoe at five o'clock. *Wang! Wang! Wang! Wanng!* So we can hoe cotton and corn. You got to chop that row one at a time. Them suckers long, them rows!

Chop out two rows a day, you know. Aw, that was all right. I didn't know any better. Want some water, have to go to the spring and get the water. Have a well, have to draw the water out the well. My daddy used to dig wells. He got two planks and lay them together. Put them in the ground. Got a bucket and let it a'whirl down in the ground and hear the water set. It go *awhoop!* Full of water, draw it up. *Doom! Doom! Doom!* Good cold water.

You want a light, you have to go get some coal oil. Two lamps sat on the mantelpiece, one lamp on each side. Them all the light you had, wadn't at all like the light nowhere. Wadn't at all like the light in the world out there. It was so dark you couldn't see nothin'. Now and then you'd see a neighbor house waaaaaay over yonder, a little old, dim light. Wadn't no light out in the country nowhere. Wadn't no gravel road, dust road.

---

[1] Sonny Boy Williamson recorded "Moonshine" in 1938 for Bluebird Records accompanied by Yank Rachell on mandolin and Joe Williams on guitar. In 1937 Sleepy John Estes recorded "Need-More Blues," which contains the expression "need-more" in place of "moonshine." Rachell is probably referring to this recording of Estes.

Well, I have done some hard work though. I used to work in the bottoms. My daddy was a timber cutter. We tote them logs. Put a big log down, two men, one man on that side, I'm on this 'un. And two men on behind.

Well, I'm a young man, but I love to pull them old men down, you know. I didn't have no better sense, strainin' myself to death. And them old men, I'd take the stick and draw it more to me you know. Put the heavy on him. The old man couldn't hardly make it. That tickled me; it tickled my dad, too. I pull him down, you know. He say, "Man, that boy sure is stout. That old boy pull me down." It was killing me. I didn't know it. But I got a kick out of pulling old men down, carryin' them logs. Yeah.

Well, the day's work done, we all be at the house. We tired, go to bed. No entertainment. We ate supper and then we go to bed. I wouldn't go out nowhere. On a Saturday, on a Sunday, we young boys would go out.

"Daddy, I want the horse."

"Oh no, them horses got to work tomorrow. You can't ride that horse."

"But now I got to work too."

"But no, you can't ride that horse; the horse got to work. You have to walk."

I walked, man. We set down and talk about the girls thereabouts the day, then go home. Well, you got to get up early that morning. The old man go in and call you once or twice. You better get up. If you don't, the next time he have a switch there. Sometimes I stomped the floor, make him think I gettin' up, you know. He come on upstairs and throw that cover back. Uh uh! You gon' get up then! Man I'm tellin' ya. Oh, I'm glad of it now, I know all about it. I'm glad it happened.

But, man, I used to follow a mule all day long. Two of 'em. Row by row. Row by row. Ten acres. Cotton. Corn. Work. Work. Work. Work. Didn't have no tractors then. No tractor wouldn't be seen. Nothin' but horses and mules.

The sun be boomin' down. See them monkeys 'cross the field jumpin'. It hot. I didn't care. All day long. Sun get to gettin' down, I get to feelin' good, get to hollerin' and singin'. Goin' out that night! And the next mornin' I wake up, I'm so sleepy. But I have to go to work. Night come, sun get low. I get to feelin' good. Gone again! I just kept a goin'. Gettin' up at four and five o'clock at mornin'. Wadn't just sunup. Just keep a goin'.

Go to work in the fields and twelve o'clock the man ring the bell. *Boom! Boom!* Go eat lunch. Ya got an hour. The day be so hot. Them old wren birds be flyin' round your door: "Laziness will kill you!" Them old birds whistling, you know, "Laziness will kill you!" That's what we said the birds was sayin'. Then the old bell go to ringing. Have to get out in that hot sun, get out in the field. Make me so mad. I said, "I'll get up and shoot that bird!"

Got sick real bad once. I was 'bout seventeen, and I had pneumonia. Thought I was dead. Went to the graveyard, lot of 'em. They told somebody I was dead. But I was sick. We live in a little old house. You know old people try to stop up every crack they see to keep warm. See, the old house is open, you know.

And the doctor, name Doctor Hess, come there say, "Open them window and door, give this boy some air or he goin' die." Say, "Y'all take all the fresh air from him, he ain't gettin' no air." That what save me, 'cause you know they breathin' my breath and it stop up. I couldn't get no air at all. It was hard on me. So they thought I was dead, but I wadn't. But I had pneumonia bad. I had it twice. I had a tetch of it when I was here in Indianapolis. But I had a bad case when I was seventeen.

My grandmother Rose. Grandfather named Horace. Rose Taylor and Horace Taylor, them my grandparents. My mother's name Lula Taylor, my father, George Rachell. At home they call me Rachel, but I'm a Rachell. Say it like this: *Ray-shell.* My grandmother started callin' me Yank. I don't know where she got it from. She called me Yank; I come up Yank. They been callin' me Yank ever since I was a little old boy. Some call me Jim, some call me black boy, some call me Rachel Road. I had all them names. Some call me baby Rachell. Some call me James, some call me S. T.

My grandparents farmed, too. That all there was to do, farm. Wadn't no factory or nothin'. Nothin' but a glove factory in Brownsville. Nobody work there but white people. No colored people work at the glove factory. I help build it, but I didn't work at it. They didn't give me no job. You had to farm. You couldn't farm, you work at a fillin' station or somethin'.

Them women would cook for them white ladies. One lady would cook for the man. She went there on the front porch and he made her go 'round to the back door. Said, "Don't come on my front porch!" Man, they was hell down there!

I left my parents on the farm when I went to town, but I would send stuff out there to help 'em out. I would take care of 'em, you know. My mother pass away before my father did. They been gone a long time now. But we were grown when she pass away. I got married and had a baby before my mother pass away. My oldest daughter, Willa B., she 'bout fifty now.

My old granddaddy, when we was kids, we used to pick at him and we run. He had an old shotgun. You have to punch cotton or somethin' in it to get it to shoot. Yeah. We go out and pick at him. Make him shoot it, then we three run, and he shoot up over our head. *Boom!*

Then grandmother would say, "Horace, you better not shoot them children!"

He say, "I'm just playin'. I ain't gonna hurt 'em."

We just carry on. Pick at him all the time.

Going to School

We lived way out in the country, so we went to school in the church, Brownsville Taylor Chapel, a Baptist church. I had three months of school. A boy didn't go to school much. They had to help their daddy work all the time. The girls went. But me, three months every year, that's all. Out in the country I had a lot of friends goin' to school, part-time, you know. But they had to go to work like I did. But the girls had a little more chance to go than the boys did, 'cause them old men wanted you to work all the time.

"Come on son, we got to cut up them corn stalks." In the corn fields where the corn grow they got a corn chopper now, but you had to take a hoe and cut them stalks down and cut them up so they'd plow over them, you know. So they'd rot under there and fertilize, you know. Something like that. Man, they had something for you to do all the time. But you could see the school bus. The white kids be goin' to school, but we'd be in the fields choppin' cotton or something.

"Hey! All the kids! I want to go!"

"No, you can't go to school. We got to fix the fence. The pasture for the horse is there. We got to go cut some dry wood to cook with. Well, you ain't got time to go to school."

Went to school a little bit, that's all. Every time I went the teacher was gone anyway. Didn't learn nothing. Well, I had a teacher, Miss Beulah, and there was an old man. Now you didn't have no desk to put your books on. You had to hold your books in your hand. I'd have a chance to go to school a little in the summer, yeah. We'd go about three days a week sometime. Well, we had to study language, grammar, geography. They had them all right. I went to the sixth grade. That's all the far I got and I was lucky to get that, 'cause I didn't have no chance to go to school.

I'd go to school with a little bucket. Got two little biscuits in it, an' a slice of meat, and go on to school. Didn't have no lot of stuff to eat. Had to walk about five miles to get to school.

Didn't have no bus to carry you to school. You got to walk there and walk back. You get home, you got to change your clothes, put on them work clothes. Go cut up a pile of wood for the house. You had to carry it into the house to keep a fire all night 'cause them houses was so raggedy you could lay in the bed and see the sunrise. That's right. I ain't lying. And you set up there and your knees burn up, get scorched trying to keep warm. Your behind will freeze if you don't turn around, 'cause there's heat in the front, but you ain't got no heat behind you. That's right.

I'd of liked to done it more, go to school. But I couldn't go, had to pick cotton. It was a good time there when I went. When I went I had a good time, yeah.

One teacher named Wiley Taylor, he was a man. Woman named Miss Beulah Hayes, and another old woman. I forget her name. She a mean old teacher. I liked Miss Beulah Hayes. She was good to us. She let you go outdoors to recess anytime. Let two of us go out to recess. Carry our apples, something to eat there, and come back in, yeah. She teach us, she had a blackboard and crayon, you know. Go up there. Me on one side, another one on the other side, and she'd mark it up. I done forgot what we did there, but we get up there, spelling, you know. Yeah, it was something else.

Church

We'd go to church. Had a wagon, two mules. We all get in the wagon and go to church. Hear the old wagon cluckin'. *Cluck-a-luck-a-luck-a-luck!* Oh, everybody have a wagon. Didn't have no air-conditioning in the church. Had the windows up. Them old ladies wear them long dresses draggin' the floor, old hat on, goin' to church.

My mother was a real serious goin'-to-church person, my mother was. Used to go to church and the preacher be preachin' toward them sinners, and they wouldn't go in. They'd peep in the window. I walk around the church many a night looking in the window. I finally decided to go in. The mournin' bench was where the sinners set, and the preacher trying to get 'em saved. All the mourners who ain't got no religion set there. So finally one night I made up my mind. I was with my mama.

She said, "Such and such a boy, his son died last week."

I said, "he did?"

"Son, you better get yourself some religion."

That scared me. The meetin' started. I went on up to the mournin' bench. The preacher, he preached and he preached. That Friday night he quit preachin'. He said, "Son, better get somebody to pray for you."

People would come up to me and say, "Son, you got it! You got it!" But I know I didn't have nothin'. I wouldn't jump, you know. I wouldn't get up.

So he said, "Get somebody you know to pray for you, son." He got tired of preachin', you know. Wadn't nobody would go up there. So I was settin' up there on the mournin' bench, but I didn't feel nothin'. He was preachin' to a bunch of us on the mournin' bench. He sat down; he said, "Son, you know somebody who will pray for you?"

I said "Yes."

Old lady settin' over in the corner, Jenny Taylor. Old man, baldheaded man, settin' over here, Duffy Taylor. Miz Jenny had a long dress draggin' on the floor, had a fan and an old bonnet on her head. I said "Miz Jenny, will you pray for me?"

She said, "Yeah."

I said, "Cousin Duffy will you pray for me?"

He said, "Yeah, son."

They come down and got on each side of me. But, boy, when them folks got through talkin', God almighty! I went up! Boy, I had it! I'm tellin' you! I got it now. I feel it, boy, I'm telling you right now. I knowed I been borned again. I know that. Then I went on there and I got it. They sprinkled me.

I come up here to Indianapolis. I join the church up here; they were Baptists. Well, the man carried me down, put me down in the water. *Blubb-blubb!* Brought me out. But I ain't like that fella that the man baptized three times. He baptized and they said, "Do you believe in it?"

He said, "Yeah." Carried him down again.

They said, "Do you believe?"

He said, "Hell, yeah! But I believe you tryin' to drown me!"[2]

I was about eleven when I first got saved.

Chapter 2

Had a pretty horse and buggy. Not no car. And I used to dress nice, you know. I'd take all them girls from them boys down there, and could play music too, you know. Them gals fell for me. My buggy be full of 'em. Dadgummit! I used to be a bad old man! My hair was black and curly and I was sharp as a tack. I went that a'way all the time.

I hitch up my buggy. If you got a field a corn, I'm gonna stop and fill my buggy up with corn for my horse. Go to the girl. Pull the bridle off the horse. Let him eat corn while I'll be in there with her. That horse eat. I come back. Get my buggy, and go home.

---

[2] This is a folktale that is documented in *American Negro Folktales*, ed. Richard M. Dorson (Greenwich, CT: Fawcett, 1968), no. 237, p. 370, "Baptizing a Hard Candidate," by Walter Winfrey.

One time, when I was a young boy, there was three, four of us run together. People used to talk about "haints," you know, ghosts. Well, I was scared of 'em; I was young. Ghosts and mad dogs, you know, I was scared of them. So we three boy had girlfriends. His girl live over here, the other 'un girl live there, and my girl live over there. So we all go together and come back together at night, 'cause it be dark. There no electric light or nothin'.

So I went on to my girl house. This boy went to his, and that one went to his. But they supposed to come by and pick me up and we all come on back together. But the bastards didn't do it that night. Left me there at my girl's house. Nine o'clock you hear them old folk movin' them chairs in they room. Now you got to go, 'cause them girls got to get up and hoe cotton in the mornin'. And you got to go home at nine o'clock, bedtime. So I settin' there, waitin' for my boys. They never did come back.

I hear the chair movin' around in there, so they gonna call bedtime directly. And he said, "Well, it's bedtime, nine o'clock y'all!"

"Yes, sir."

I take my hat. Now I'm scared. She said, "You scared?"

I said, "Uh uh!"

She look and see my hair was standin' straight up on my head, I was so scared. I had to go get out in that dark road and try to go home by myself 'cause my buddies, they done gone. Well, goin' to my girl's house on my way back is a graveyard. I was scared of a graveyard then. And a gate open up there at the graveyard. And that gate were wide open. And I know I had to go by that graveyard. I couldn't get home no other way. And I had to leave them folk's house. Man, I was scared! And in the thicket you hear rabbits and them runnin' at night. Dark! Moon, sometime it shine and then run past a cloud. You know how that does.

So I go on. Well, I didn't want to pass that graveyard. I stood there and I stood there. But I got to go by that graveyard to get home. I stood there, so I made up my mind to go up there a piece. Was some guys that went in the man's field and stole some roastin' ear. They carried it up in the graveyard to count out the ears, how many who got and how many got the other 'un. Well, I hear one say, "You got this 'un, you take that 'un."

I said, "That's God and the devil countin' out souls."

One said, "You take this 'un. I take this 'un." Well, there they went in the gate. One of 'em drop an ear of corn, you know. Other one say, "I'm short of a ear of corn." Said, "I'm short of one." Well, I'm the one at the gate. Wanted to pass the gate. He said, "Yeah? Well, you get that one at the gate."

Well, I thought they talkin' about me. When he said, "Get that one at the gate," man, I pass that gate runnin' so fast. You see my foot so often you thought I was crawlin'. I run half a mile! And I got to a fork in the road there. And so there's a big tree there where we boys always go and chunk at folks goin' by. Well, I done got by that graveyard and I want a blow. I'm tired.

I say, "Whew!"

The old man behind the tree, he were there. He see me.

He say, "Whew!"

And I say, "What is that?" I go, "Whew," and he go, "Whew," again.

He say, "We sure done run, have we?"

I say "Hell no, we ain't run that much. Now we gonna run!"

I lit out again.[1] Boy, I run home. Run through the wire fence. Told my daddy to open the door. He so slow open the door. I kickin' on the door so he open it.

"What the matter with you, fool?"

I say, "Somethin' at me"

"What at you?"

From then on I don't go with no boy to no girl's house and have them leave me, 'cause I'm scared of a graveyard. I'd come by one on my horse, I'd shut my eye till I passed it. I was that scared of a graveyard. But it's funny some things you think you can see. I know that. Some kind of things I don't know. Maybe it 'magination. So I just don't know what to think sometime. Yessir, I have a big round of my life that I can think of.

I used to go huntin'. I used to work for a man who run a dry goods store. And I worked for a lawyer, Joe Mann. He had a pump gun. I'd hunt with it

---

[1] This story has elements of different folktales that are common to many cultures, where a ghost haunts the burial ground. In some, boys are dividing nuts or they are sheep thieves; listeners outside the cemetery wall think the boys are the devil and the Lord dividing the souls and leave at full speed. See Stith Thompson's six-volume *Motif Index of Folk-Literature* (Bloomington: Indiana University Press, 1955).

all the time. I hunt rabbit. That's all I wanted, rabbit. Had a dog. If he didn't catch a rabbit we'd whup him. If you cut the hair off a dog's head and put it under your doorstep, he'd stay at home. He wouldn't leave.

See, my daddy would go to town in the wagon, every Saturday. He'd come back with some old dog followin' him back. Look back and there was some old dog. We'd catch him, cut the hair off his head so he wouldn't leave. Then we'd go huntin' with him. Sometime we'd catch ten rabbit a day. That's true. Yeah, them big old swamp rabbits. We hunt rabbit all season. Now one season rabbit got worm in him. Well, if he got a worm in him we turn him a'loose. If he ain't got a worm in him we'd eat him.

Go to town, you go on a wagon. Two mule and a board 'cross there on the seat. Settin' up there on the seat board. Be about twelve mile from the farm to Brownsville. You and the horses goin' to town. Every now and then, you might see a T model, somebody in a T model or somethin'. There wadn't no car much. Horses was ever scare of a car.

Shoot! Maaan! These folk got it made now. Don't have to go outdoor for nothin' here. Turn a button, lights come on all over everywhere. Turn a button, water come on. You didn't have that down there. Had to go pack your water. Woman get ready to iron, you put the iron 'fore the fireplace. Then it get hot. Then take it out. Tetch it and see how hot it is. Iron your clothes. Didn't have no, shoot! Didn't have nothin', man! Had an old flat stove to get your iron hot. Iron your clothes and everything. But they went nice and clean. They wore them old overalls, four button, them old, long overalls. Women had to get down, wash them. Weren't no washing machine. Women wash them with their hand, all day long. Hang 'em out on the line. You have to go out to the outhouse. Don't matter how cold it is. Now they don't have to go outdoor for nothin', the kids. They don't know nothin' about that, all the children. I tell them that at school. They look at me like a fool. They think I'm lyin', but I ain't. It's true. I been through all that.

Chapter 3

I was 'bout eight. I went down a dusty road one day. Man had a house settin' on the side to the road. Well, he settin' on his porch playin' this mandolin. I went by and asked him what it was.

"This a mandolin, son."

"I like that. Let me see it."

He said, "All right."

I give it a lick or two. I give it back to him, say, "I sure like it."

"Let me sell it to you."

"What you take for it?"

"Five dollar."

Now five dollar, I didn't have no five dollar. My daddy didn't either. I couldn't dream of five dollar.

I said, "I ain't got that, Mr. Augie." Man's name was Augie Rawls. My parents knowed him, but I didn't want to tell my parents he sold it to me.

Said, "I got a pig I'll trade for it."

"You got a pig?"

"Yeah."

"Where the pig?"

I said, "At home."

"Well, all right. Go get the pig. I'll let you have the mandolin."

My mother give me a little pig, you know. She said, "James, raise you that pig and you'll have some meat this fall to eat."

I said, "Yes'm."

I went on home. Went to the barn. My daddy raised plenty corn. I shell some corn and put it down there. I called the little pig out and he went to eatin' corn. I got me a croaker sack and caught the little pig and put 'im in there. Went 'round the thicket and carried that pig to the man's house. He took the pig. He like this pig, a little old black china, a fine-blooded hog. He knowed what the value of the pig would be when it growed up. But I didn't. I didn't care.

I went on home with the mandolin. *Blam, blam, blam.* Couldn't play nothin'. Just bammin' on it. It sound good to me, you know. It was somethin' new to me. A guitar wadn't new, but a mandolin was new to me. *Blam, blam, blam.* I just liked the sound of it. Had eight strings on it, and I enjoyed it. I didn't know one sound from the other, but I know I liked it. It had stripes down the back. Was a gourd mandolin, round in the back. What they call a 'tater-bug mandolin.

It's a worrisome thing when somebody playin' and can't play nothin' on it. It run you crazy. *Blam, blam, blam.* Well, I wadn't playin' nothin'. Didn't know nothin' to play.

My daddy, he sit and listen to me awhile. The old man got tired. He short winded.

"Here, son, put that thing down. Gotta go to work tomorrow."

"All right, sir."

I put it down. He get up and go to work. I get up and, as soon as he leave, I get it and go to workin' on it!

Mother'll go along with you for a long time. Finally one mornin' she come down the stairs, down by the fireplace.

"James?"

I say, "Ma'm."

"Where that pig of yours?"

"I don't know, Mama. I reckon he out there."

She said, "I ain't seed that pig in a day or two."

"I ain't either, Mama." I just kept bammin' on the mandolin, you know.

She said, "You ain't seen 'im in a day or two?"

"No."

"Well, go see you can find that pig."

"Yes'm."

I put the mandolin down. I didn't want to go, but I had to go out there. I went out to the barn. Stood there about ten minutes. I didn't stay long enough to fool her. But I was young. I didn't have no sense. I wanted to get back on that mandolin. I'm goin' back and get that mandolin. Come on back.

"James, you see that pig anywhere?"

"No, Mama, I ain't seed that pig nowhere."

"Where'd you go."

"Man, I went all around the thicket and everywhere."

"You a liar. You ain't been gone that long."

Uh oh! I kept bammin' on the mandolin. I wadn't studyin' her.

She says, "What is that thing?"

I said, "A mandolin."

"Mandolin?"

"Yes'm."

"Where you get if from? Did you steal it?"

You better not steal something; them old folks'll kill you. Better not steal in them days. Better not steal nothin'.

I said, "No, Mama I didn't steal it."

"Well, where you get it from, then?"

"Oh, Mama, I got it from a fella."

"What fella?"

"Oh, Mama, I got it from a man. I don't know his name."

Well, I didn't want to tell her Mr. Augie Rawls had it, 'cause he were a friend to my peoples, you know. I know they'd get at him and make me carry the mandolin back and get the pig. I wouldn't tell her.

She said, "You don't know the man's name?"

"Oh, no, Mama, I don't know the man's name."

"And he let you have that?"

I said, "Yes'm."

She didn't say nothin'. She was sewin'. Put her needle and thread down. A big willow tree was in the front yard. I know where she was goin'. She went out the door. She went there, got every switch on that tree, that tree willow. She come in there.

"Uh huh, you gonna tell me where you got it from? I'm gonna whup you," she said. "Pull off them clothes. I ain't gonna wear them clothes out. I bought 'em. I'm gonna whup the meat."

I had to tell her then. I said, "Mama I traded that pig for this mandolin."

"I ought to kill you," she said. "I'm not gonna whup you, boy. But you know what? This fall when we butcher meat and eat it, you eat that thing, 'cause you ain't gonna get no meat."

I didn't care. I had the mandolin.

Well, a long time later on, a white friend of mine, his mother had an old mandolin. He made some pig ears and put 'em on it, 'cause I traded a pig for the mandolin. He took the mandolin to me, one of them old, gold mandolins, striped, like the first kind of mandolin I started to playin'. I kept it a long time, but, movin' and all, I don't know what 'come of it. That was about three years ago.

Don't many people play the blues on a mandolin. I can't play like I used to. Arthritis got my fingers all crooked up, stiff and everything. But I strum along sometime. Yeah, it's been a long time ago.

Chapter 4

I lived in the country and my uncle Bud, Uncle Dan Taylor, lived in the city. He'd come out on the weekend and play for us. He used to play guitar some and we was small and young. We were glad to hear what he played. I don't know if it was good or not. He played old blues, back home. We'd enjoy him playing and he'd teach us a little, and so we'd start to playing. And he'd go back, and we'd try to play after what he played.

I knowed some girls who had a guitar, three sisters. We three brother would borrow that guitar and we would go to playin' it and we learned to play on it. We wadn't tryin' to court them girl back then. We was too young for that.

My older brother started, and he'd teach me and I'd teach the baby boy. So we all could play, all three of us.

My cousin Henry Taylor was a good guitar player; he could beat Uncle Bud, Daniel, playing. He could play some guitar! I didn't play guitar with Henry. He was wild. He didn't stay around us much. Uncle Bud would come and see us all the time, but Henry, he stay gone a lot of times.

Henry Taylor, yeah. He went to the penitentiary. He went and took the light off the railroad track. They sent him to the pen for it.

I was raised way out in the country, but there was a lot of music goin' around. People sing hymns in church and you could hear people singing in the fields. You could hear them hollerin' and singing. I don't see how they done it in that hot sun, but I guess it felt good. You'd get to sweatin' so much that cool you off. Be so hot you see them monkeys jumpin' through the field. Hell yeah, that's right! See something jumpin' through the field!

A man had an old grafeyphone and everybody go to his house. It wasn't but a few people who had one, old grafeyphone with a horn on the thing. You had to wind it up and it played. Well, we go out and set on his porch and listen to him playin' that thing. He had all kind of old music on there, so we heard a record, Bessie Smith, Lemon Jefferson, and all of them.

And I get that in my head. So I go back and get the mandolin and try make the mandolin say that. Which I do. I make my mandolin say everything I said. So I kept on till I learn how to make a note or two on it.

And Willie Newbern come through there, and he know about a mandolin more'n I did. Well, he kind of played some. That give me an idea how to play some. So he started me off. He played some; then I got to playin'. The more I play, the more it come to me. So, then, I hear records and thing. I go play and try to play like the record, till I learn how to play it.

First tune I learn to play, "Wonder would a matchbox hold my clothes? I ain't got so many, but I got so far to go." That's what I played on the mandolin and on the guitar, too. I learn the guitar before I play the mandolin, so what I play on the guitar I tried to play on the mandolin, see. And that just kept me a'goin'. "Send for whiskey, she brought me gasoline. That's the meanest woman I ever seen."[1] That's the song I was singin'. That's part of that

---

[1] Blind Lemon Jefferson recorded "Match Box Blues" in 1927. The "Send for whiskey" verse occurred in Tommy Johnson's 1928 "Cool Drink of Water Blues." The second guitar by Charlie McCoy was played like a mandolin. These are traditional lyrics, so they could have reached Rachell through oral tradition. Rachell would have been 17 or 18 years old when these records were released, whereas he seems to be speaking here of a younger age level. Perhaps he has projected later songs (derived from the records) back to his earliest learning experience because these are the earliest songs he can actually remember.

song. I made that 'un up, I didn't hear it from nobody else. I play it on the guitar and then on the mandolin, and that carried me on.

I used to play the banjo some. I used to play the harmonica. I quit all of that. Used to play guitar. I don't play nothin' but a mandolin now. You can't play all them things and be good at none of them. Yeah, I used to play old country blues. That's what I play now. The old down-home, country blues 'cause I borned with the blues.

Willie Newbern come through Brownsville; he was a mandolin player. He was older than I was. He played some, so I caught some from him. He went to Memphis and they raided a joint somewhere he was playin' in. They carried him to jail, and they wanted him to go on the road on a chain gang and he wouldn't go. And I think they killed him because he wouldn't go out on the highway to work. He was a good musician, but he wouldn't go out there.[2]

Yeah, Hambone Willie Newbern. I don't know where he was from, but he'd come through Brownsville and hang around. He was a good guitar player and mandolin player. And Bob Stevens was too, I knowed both of them. I was playin' mandolin before I knowed him, but I knowed some of his stuff.

I didn't have no way of tunin' the mandolin aright till Willie Newbern come through there, and he showed me how to tune it. In natural, that's how I tune it, 'cause a lot of 'em tune it in crosstune. But I don't. You can tune it, play another way on it. But it ain't the natural way. But the natural you can play anything in the same key. But you tune it crosstune, you got to tune it over when you play somethin' else. But if you play the natural you can play anything you want, you don't have to tune it over.

John Estes know Willie Newbern 'fore I did. So he come through Brownsville, Willie Newbern did, had a guitar and mandolin on his arm. Carry both of 'em. He could play both of 'em. Now I see him with the mandolin and I got with it. I learn a lot of tune from him, he learn somethin' from me. But I learned more tune from him than he did from me, 'cause he knowed more of

---

[2] In the article "Yank Rachell in Lousiville," in *Blues Unlimited* (November 1963, pp. 3–4), Paul Garon states that Hambone Willie Newbern "died in the workhouse in Shelby County."

'em. He was older than I was. Willie Newbern, he a tall, dark fella. Was a black fella. He a guitar man though!

PLAYING MUSIC IN THE COUNTRY

So I go to the little suppers out in the country. So I went back there. I kept my mandolin. Walked about a mile and a half to play, to a man's house. He had a party. I couldn't play nothin' much, but played somethin'. The man gave me fifty cents. Lord, that was some money them days for me! Fifty cents! Yeah, I thought the man was crazy, payin' me. I brought it back home and told my mama.

"Mama, I have fifty cents."

Said, "You need more 'n that."

I don't know what I played there, some kind of blues, I guess. It's been so long I can't hardly remember that stuff. I was about ten or twelve when I earned that first fifty cent playing the mandolin.

On Saturday I play all night. We'd play at night thereabouts and then come home and go to the fields in the daytime. My brother play guitar and mandolin. I play mandolin. And my other brother play guitar. Sometime, somebody play washboard for rhythm.

People gave house parties. Like in the kitchen women be in there cookin', with the table across the middle of the door. They be in there cookin' catfish. They'd sell it. And we be out there playin'. People be in there dancin'. They did the Charleston, and Gettin'-over-Sally or something, belly rubbin'. They be dancin' till some guy get mad and shoot in the house. Shoot the lamp out. It happened, oh yeah! One night Sleepy John and I had to run off. He got hung up on a barbwire fence. Every Friday and Saturday night somebody be givin' a house party. Some people be out in the barn shootin' craps.

They givin' a supper; you go over there and drink plenty white whiskey, jug o' white whiskey, bootleggin'. Police be under the house tryin' to catch you with it. Yeah, tryin' to catch you drinkin'. One tried to catch me one day. I see him comin' round the house. I throwed the bottle away. He couldn't get no proof on me. He couldn't do nothin' about it.

Sometimes we played for white people. Play that waltz and fox-trot, you know, "You Are My Sunshine," "Turkey in the Straw," ragtime pieces, "Bugle Call Rag." I played them for them. They didn't do too much drinkin'. Mostly they'd dance and have a good time. But the blues, they didn't know nothin' about that. They didn't know no blues.

Chapter 5

I don't know exactly how old I was when we met, I and Sleepy John. But I was a man. I was grown. Charles Bonds, he give a supper three night a week, Wednesday, Thursday, and Friday. Man bought me a guitar to play for him. I didn't have one then. I would go around and play for him every weekend.

He had them midnight parties. He'd buy fish and put the table across the kitchen door. The women be in there cooking fish and chicken and all that. They all be in there dancin' and have a good time, sippin' that moonshine, white whiskey. Sometime there be so many people they broke the floor in.

Well, just like I was livin' east, John Estes was livin' north, from Brownsville, out in the country. So in them days, in town, you heard tell somebody can play over there, you going go over there and play with him, see can you beat him, you know. Something like that. So I was playin'. John heard about me; he hadn't never saw me. So one night some friend brought John there. Said, "Man, we go to the supper tonight. Old Yank gonna be over there." Say, "He a guitar player, you know." And John was a guitar player too. He couldn't play so good, but he was a good songster. So, I was settin' up there. So, he come in at night. Well, we gonna play against one another. We didn't know one another. We gonna buck up 'gainst one another. He come on in; he set down and listen. I looked at him, a long, tall fella, kind of cockeyed. He come in there and set down. I played and he played. And he playin' pretty good, and I went and played again.

So we got to playin' together and I told him I played mandolin too. He said, "You can? I can't play no mandolin." So the next night I brought my mandolin. And he went to playin' behind me and I'm playin' the mandolin. Then we team up. Play together forty years, I and Sleepy John. We train a lot of guys, brought up under us. We the first one made a record in the South then. First colored boys. Yeah.[1]

I was still workin' in the fields when we met. I was playin' around Brownsville by myself till we met one another. We got acquainted and then we started to playin' together. We practice and play together all the time, so then we have a little band in Brownsville: Eric Bridey, Pie Gandy, Jim Davis, myself, and Sleepy John. Jim Davis playin' bass horn, Eric Bridey playin' the fiddle, Pie Gandy playin' trombone, John playin' the guitar, and I'm playin' the mandolin. We had a five-piece band. Played some old-time songs, some old blues.

We played together for about five or six years. Some of them died out and quit playin', you know. But me and John stayed together. And some of 'em was in a car wreck; it killed some of 'em. They was goin' to play somewhere that night. I wadn't with 'em and John wadn't with 'em. Oil truck, or something, hit 'em, killed 'em. Killed 'bout two of 'em.

Chapter 6

I went to town when I got grown, when I got eighteen. I left Mama and them out there in the country, but I would send them stuff back and come see about them. I left there and decided to work on the railroad. I just got tired of farming.

---

[1] Rachell and Estes were obviously not the first to record in the South. He probably means the first to record from around Brownsville. However, this still isn't accurate. Hambone Willie Newbern recorded in March 1929, six months before Rachell and Estes. Pearl Dixon from Somerville recorded in 1927, and Noah Lewis, from around Henning, Tennessee, recorded with Gus Cannon in 1928.

I went to work for the railroad. I put my age up. The man wouldn't hire you to work on the railroad then, lessen you were twenty-one. Told you you had to go through a lot of tape. I told him I was twenty-one. But I look like a man. I look like I was twenty-five, 'cause I was big, you know, and stout, so they went and hire me. Work 'bout a year on the railroad.

Then I went to town and stayed around town and worked there. Worked at them filling stations, garage, barbecue. Worked that barbecue. I'm a barbecue man now! I worked on the highway for a while. Guy come through there building highway and he hired me. He had a bunch there and they was payin' good. We go out there and set on the bank every day, goin' to get a job with him. He told me, "Well, you have to come out here. I don't know; I may could hire you." Finally he hired me and I helped put down a highway, till he got ready to leave, go out of town, and I wouldn't go out of town with him.

And I come back home, and I go to work at a fillin' station driving a wrecker truck for a man, pullin' people out of ditches and things. I worked for Henry Bracken. He had a big garage in Brownsville. And I worked at a cafe. Two, three cafe I worked at.

And the last man I worked for, Frank Richard, he had a coffeehouse in the hotel in Brownsville. The barbecue man rented a place in the hotel and had a barbecue stand in there. Well, I cook barbecue for him.

On a Saturday them colored guy come to town. Well, them skin would be good and crusty. Frank Richard say, "Hell, Rachell. You take the skin and sell 'em." But now I had to sell 'em out the window. They couldn't come in. There was restaurants that said "White only" and some said "Colored." They were hard on black people down there!

Yeah, town be full of 'em. They come out, "Hey, you got any skin?" I say, "Yeah." I make that hot sauce and put it over the skin, you know. And they come out and I sell it! Well, I sold so many of 'em, he got jealous. He said, "Hell, you sellin' more skin than I'm sellin' meat!" Yeah, them skins was good!

I'd eat at home rather than eat that barbecue. I get tired of cookin' that and eating it. But I cook six and seven shoulder at once. I go home and eat.

Had a lady in there; she goin' to watch the barbecue. I was off that day and the whole pit caught on fire and the hotel caught on fire. Fire wagon come there and messed up the hotel; the man had to leave.

Worked as a chauffeur. I used to drive around town there. I didn't go out of town. Another guy used to drive 'em to Chicago and places. I just drive from house to house. I worked for white people driving. They had a big car. See, I was working for a white lady, Miss Gertrude Fox. Boy have to wear them leather gloves, high boots. She have a car telephone in the back and I take 'em out to their friends' house to play bridge, or something. I don't know what they done. Had a chauffeur cap on and everything, and the colored girls would be on the street taking care of their babies. The whole street be full of little girls taking care of little babies for them, you know. And I take them out, you know.

"James, pick me up at three o'clock."

"Yes Ma'am." But see, after you eat, I'd be sportin' around in that sweet little car. And them babes were talkin' to me, you know, and all of that stuff.

WORKING ON THE RAILROAD

Workin' on the railroad, I had my music with me on the boxcar. And we go, like if it was a Sunday, Saturday night, we have to leave, go where we goin' to work at that Monday. Well, I have my music with me. I play for the boys when we settin' down there, till I come back. And when have a play, I go on and make the play, go play for a dance on the weekend somewhere and then go back to the railroad camp. We had bunks, one sleep here, one on top, and one on the other one. Had a cook.

I worked for a puttin'-up-fence gang, fencin' the side of the railroad. The railroad company build a fence side the railroad track on each side 'cause people would take old horses and cows and put 'em on the track for the train to kill 'em, so they get paid for it. See that? They'd take an old, poor horse and he'd see a train comin' and he'd go out the way. That train kill 'em and then they'd have to sue the company for 'em. Because the railroad was payin' out so much money, well, the railroad got tired of that. They went and build a fence on each side of the track, big ball of wire, from Brownsville to Paris, Tennessee. That's as far as I went with 'em. Diggin' post holes; rollin' out wire; building fences. I'd line up the fence, line up posts, and then nail them posts. Dig them post holes all the way, from Memphis to Paris, Tennessee. That where I put 'em down at. Yessir. Had a whole streetcar full of 'em, me and another guy. I was big then. We'd yank the suckers off the truck.

And on the side of the railroad, you didn't go round that creek; you had to go through there, put that fence up. We went through a wood. Lot o' snake there. Had one boy go along with a stick killin' snakes.

So I was settin' out in the woods eatin' lunch under a tree and I smelled somethin'. I look and there was a snake. Had a spot in its face and he as big as your leg. And I call the boy, "Man, here's a snake." He come down, hit him three time with an ax before he killed him. That sucker flutter big. I said, "Uh uh. I ain't workin' here no more." I left there and I ain't went back on no railroad no more. Got my clothes and left there. Uh uh. No sir. Why I so scared of snakes? I don't know. I'm scared of anybody's not scared of snakes. That's how scared I am. Yeah, you run into everything on the side of the railroad. You go through them thickets; wade water to your waist; put that fence through there. You didn't go 'round with that fence, had to go through there.

Then we go to the boxcar. Go to whuppin' around one another and joke with one another. So I joked a old boy one night. I was layin' on my bunk. I was talkin' about his mammy. And I didn't think no more about it. And before I knowed it he was standin' over me cryin' with a double-blade ax. Said, "I'm gonna cut your goddamn throat, son of a bitch. You talkin' about me."

I said, "Man, we just playin'. You don't want to cut me." Say, "I'm your friend, man." Now I got a thirty-eight under my head, but I couldn't get it. So he finally went on away. He laid down; I got up with mine. Said, "Son of a bitch, I'm goin' kill you."

"I didn't kill you. Why you goin' kill me?" We just actin' the fool, that's all, 'cause he coulda killed me and I coulda killed him.

So I had my music on the boxcar. I play music for 'em. We have a big time. Go to them little old town. Go out there to them people house and everything. Old man caught me one time in a little old coal-stop town, 'fore we get to Memphis. He had some pretty girl there. So I played there that night. Old gal must have told the man I was comin' back. We all say goodnight. I'm gonna slip 'round by the window. I slip 'round to the window. I look up; he said, "You ain't gone yet?"

I said, "No. I ain't gone yet, but I'm goin' now." I didn't go back there no more. That old gal is tricky. Fool me. I sure want to get in that house and see that gal. I was crazy, young. I didn't care. Oh, yeah, I like them women. I'd fool around.

Well, I had a pretty good time in Brownsville, pretty good hard time. I worked there so hard. I worked at a cafe, fillin' station, garage, and everywhere, barbecue, cookin', on a farm. I done 'em all.

Chapter 7

We was living in Memphis, I and Sleepy John. We had a jug band; call it the Three Js.: John, James, and Jab. Jab Jones a piano player, and he play jug with us out on the street. One day Jab come by and he said, "There's a man here makin' records from New York." Say, "Why don't you come up there and see can you make a record with him. He on Short Beale."

I said, "All right, tomorrow we'll meet you up there." I thought he was lyin' to me, until me and John went on and sure enough there was Mr. Peer settin' up there from New York. We played a piece or two. He said, "I can use you'all." We went on and recorded. In them times they didn't have no tape; they had wax, and that wax was expensive. You couldn't mess up that wax and erase it like you do this tape, anyway.

Ralph Peer. Oh, man, that's way back! A big, fine white guy. Fat, good-lookin' white fella. That was in '29. He paid us three boys nine hundred dollars! I thought he was crazy. I was just out of the country. Didn't know much about no money. Young, didn't have no family to take care of or nothin'. I done messed that up. But I learned a lot.

Noah Lewis was there. He play a piece too, Noah Lewis. He was all right. He could play harmonica. He blow it through his nose, some of it. I ain't saw that before. He was older than I was. I don't know exactly how much, but a lot older. He was from Ripley, Tennessee.

We played some with Jab Jones after that record. Jab was a good piano player. He played good with us on that record. He died 'bout two year after we made that record together. Heard he drinked himself to death. He was about our age. He was a heavy built, dark, brown-skinned fellow.[1]

Exchange and Front Street, that where we were.[2] I forget the name of the studio. Man, 1929, that's a lot of years ago, you know. I'm eighty-six; I can't think of all a that stuff. But anyway, we three, the man give us 'bout three hundred dollar apiece. But we made several records. Just give it away. We didn't know. We was glad to get that anytime. That was real good money. I'm just from the country and didn't know nothin' about no money, hell no.

We went down on Beale Street, me and John. We bought some of them old secondhand suits and shoes. We bought three whole suits. Hired us a taxi to go up to Arkansas. Kept the man there a week ridin' us around. Stayed over there and played. Had all that money; went to Arkansas and blow it all, in several days. Hell, we didn't know what to do with it. Spend it all.

Got back to Memphis. Well, I'm sixty miles from Memphis to Brownsville. I had my brother's wristwatch. When I got back to Memphis I had to pawn the wristwatch to get back to Brownsville. Done got spent all a that money. You know, money and fools don't mix.

Then in Brownsville, the record come out. Well, the police had to come run 'em off the sidewalk and unblock the street from listenin' at that record. 'Cause that was our hometown, you know. And the man had a music store there, you know, Arthur Johnson. And he play them records on a Saturday. And it be like that, them runnin' all over one another tryin' to hear our record. Well, it was something to me. I thought it was great to hear myself! 'Cause I had never done nothin' like that. Just out of the country, I didn't know.

---

[1] Jab Jones also recorded with the Picaninny Jug Band in 1932 and the Memphis Jug Band in 1934.

[2] Exchange and Front Street in Memphis was the location of the Ellis Auditorium, which has since been demolished. The Victor Master Book confirms that this was where all of the 1929–30 Victor sessions in which Rachell participated were recorded.

Arthur Johnson said, "That record brought you all half a million dollars." And we got about three hundred. Yeah, I just give away a lot of dough. I didn't understand. If I had the money that I was supposed to get, I'd be a multimillionaire right now.

But I didn't get it. We didn't know how! We didn't know what we were doin'. They just beat us out the money 'cause we young country fools. Just glad to get to make some record. I got so much royalty comin', but it got messed up. I can't get it. Didn't have nobody pullin' for me, show me nothin' about it. I didn't have no education or nothin'. Just had a little mother wit. Didn't go to school or nothin', get no education. I don't have no education even now.

But music just come to me. Music's in my head. I pick up that mandolin now, I can match up a song and sing it. You never heard it. You wouldn't know if it's right or not. But I would know. Right now. I play a song now. What is it? I'll put a name to it. Just like I'm gonna do tomorrow night.

Boy want me to help him cut a record. I'm gonna go out there, help him cut it, and put a name to the song. That's all it is. That's all's to it. It's come to ya. I never go to no studio with no papers, readin' and this and that. No. Don't need it. But not everybody can do that. I can't do a lot like I used to, 'cause my brain ain't together.

We made some good song on that record, back in 1929. Sleepy John, Jab Jones, and I did. We play "Divin' Duck Blues." Well, John and I wrote that. We made it up. "If the river was whiskey, I was a diving duck, dive to the bottom, never would come up." We'd match this song, ram 'em together, you know. So it went big, "Divin' Duck Blues." A big hit song.

And we put out "Black Mattie Blues." We made that up. "Hey Black Mattie, where you stay last night? Come home this mornin, your clothes ain't fittin' right. Wake up big mama, get your big leg offa me. May be good to you, but I swear you mashin' me." There was a girl I always call Black Mattie. That's a woman, you know. That's all.

"Expressman Blues," that's a song I made up in the studio. "Expressman, you done me wrong. You moved my baby from me when I was away from home." That how it start.

Me and Sleepy John wrote "Stack o' Dollars." "I got a stack o' dollars as long as I am tall. If you be my woman, baby, you can have them all." We had to rhyme 'em up, you know. Put something to 'em.

Sleepy John made a lot of songs. He like to make songs about all the people he know in Brownsville. One song was "Al Rawls." Al Rawls an undertaker in Brownsville. I got a niece working there now, Ruby. She been there for twenty years. He got his own graveyard. There's a big family of 'em. Them Rawls pretty well-to-do people.

'Nother song was "Lawyer Clark." Yeah. A lawyer in Brownsville, Huey Clark. Best lawyer they said, keep ya out of jail. He'd book John out of jail a lot of times, 'cause John get drunk every holiday and go to jail. They wouldn't make him pay nothin'. Let him out when he get sober. He used to write a song about all those people.

"Freedom Bank" a song about a bank that had special low-cost loans. John could make up some of the most crazy song that I ever heard. John make up a song about anything, settin' here right now. He write a song right now. 'Fore you know it he done. Way he do it. Some of his song I don't know. We wadn't together all the time.

John wadn't no real guitar player, but he was a good songster. People ride ten mile on a horse just to hear him sing. You could hear him singin' near downtown. He'd shut his eye and cross his leg twice. Cross his leg this a'way and then bring that foot under there. And then have that gallon, half-gallon whiskey settin' there. And he gon' play some music then. And they know he would.

They come on, "Hey, John!"

"Hi, got a drink?"

"Yeah! Play me some juicy thing, John!"

"All right."

Bring your whiskey in there and that sucker go to singin'. God knows. Tear the roof off the house!

Chapter 8

I played with a guy called Son Brimmer in Memphis, a jug band. John, John didn't fool with 'em. Didn't make no record with him. I just played with him some.

The name was Will Shade, but we call him Son Brimmer. He play guitar so hard there a print of his guitar in his finger, he mash those strings so hard. He play some with Gus Cannon, blow a jug. Long time! But I remember some of it!

I was in the Three Js jug band in Memphis when I made the record in 1929. Another guy played jug named Ham Lewis. He would bust a jug, bust it open playin' it.

Hammie Nixon come up with me and John. Hammie ridin' around tryin' to learn how to play when I and John were playin'. Hammie learned to play harp behind me and that mandolin. Then we played together. Then Hammie took up the jug. He went playin' jug and I was playing guitar and mandolin. John playin' guitar. So, we call it the Tornado Jug Band. Well, Hammie played jug and a harp. He'd play the harp a while; then he'd quit playin' harp and blow a jug. Well, me and John would be playin' with him.

I didn't play steel guitar, just an old wooden guitar. In Memphis, late at night, we'd go to the white people house. Get up on the porch; go to playin'. *Blum! Blum! Blum!* Well, they liked it, some of 'em. They come to the door and give us some money and make us welcome. And people upstairs in them 'partments throwin' money down to us. And a boy had the jug. We had so many nickels and dimes in that jug, it stopped it up. He couldn't blow it. That's the truth.

We'd do that every night, thereabouts in different places. Yeah. Sometime we'd go places and they tell us, "We got death in our house, sickness." We go over somewhere else, play. But they liked it. Twelve o'clock we'd go to the folks' house. Wonder they hadn't killed all of us.

But every weekend we'd go somewheres out and play. And sometimes everybody ask John about playin' on a Friday night and he'd tell 'em, "Yeah."

So, one night he told a fella we gonna play for him but we didn't. We played for the other fella. So the fella come there with a pistol, goin' to make us quit playin' for the other fella and go to his place. He said, "Man, I done bought all that fish and stuff, you told a damn lie!" Said, "You gonna play for me tonight."

But this other man done give us a little more money, so we went to him. Hell, we weren't foolin'. So this man run us away from there.

I said, "John," I said, "you quit bookin' all them places." I said, "You quit." He said, "Well, man, you know it's more money."

I say, "Yeah, but you can't do that."

Go ahead a week or two more, the same thing come up. Guy come there, "Hey! Man, I done bought all that fish and stuff and you ain't goin' play. Hell, a crowd there." The crowd goin' follow where the music was, the best of the music. So we had that kind of trouble. But me and Sonny Boy didn't have that kind of trouble. 'Cause John tell anybody yeah, he'd play for 'em, and know he ain't gonna play. He done booked somebody else, but he'll book both the places, so if we don't get one, we get the other 'un. See, John wanted more money.

Hoboing

Sleepy John and I played in Kentucky, in Paducah, in a little old cafe up there, but I can't remember now. Yeah. We hoboed together. We'd catch a freight train. Like we go. Train be makin' up; we wait for it. And train start out; some boxcar have a flat. Won't be nothin' but that flatcar you know. Well, we can catch it. Train start up. Sometime we throw our music on this one and get back on the other car and ride it, and ride and ride, till we get somewhere and we get off.

One time we rode, the man switch the boxcar off and locked it. And we in there and the train pull off. They left us on the switch. And we couldn't get out. We knockin' and bammin' and bammin'. Then the man come by and pick the car up, so we got out. But he left us in there for a day. We thought we wadn't never gonna get outta there. So we quit gettin' in them boxcars like that. We hobo to a place and we get out. We didn't have much money. We'd buy some candy and crackers. Eat candy and soda cracker, you know, drink a lot of water, and we'd find somewhere to eat, some good food to eat. Yeah, we hobo a lot of time.

Sleepy John knowed people way back in the country. We go way back there to play. He know 'em. I didn't know 'em. Well, we had a string band, so he'd get us to play down there. We all go down there and play with him and he get drunk. They get that old gallon o' white whiskey. He drink that whiskey and he get drunk. And we band boys there together. He go against us, and we all get into it. He wouldn't go back with us, so we go on leave him down there. Then next week he come home. "Man, I got drunk. I got drunk, man." Well, we ain't payin' no attention.

Everything work out all right, most time, 'cept one night. Sleepy John' cousin cut my face. We was out drivin' home from playin' at a juke joint, I and John were. And his cousin and girlfriend were in the back seat. We stopped by the roadside and drink that moonshine. Well, Sleepy John's cousin got jealous. He think the girlfriend like me. Well, maybe she did. So he reach over from the back seat and cut my face with a razor. Man, I'm tellin' you. I chase that sucker out of the car. Run down the road, blood comin' from my face. I find a old railroad spike layin' in the road and when I catch him, *whup!* Beat his head in. Left him lyin' in the road and went on. Never heard about him again. Boy cut my face! I got that scar today.

But I and Sleepy John go all around together. Played the little towns and the big 'uns. Bells, Tennessee, Humboldt, Milan, Trenton, played in all them little town 'round there.

Chapter 9

I used to date Memphis Minnie's sister. Sometime I play with her—not in no club, just go to her house sometime and play. She live in Memphis and we'd be by there and drop by her house. You know, go in and a jammin' with 'em, or something like that. I didn't do no recordin' with her, or nothin' like that. Last time I saw her, me and Hammie Nixon went to her home and played her a piece. That was years ago though. After then I heard next thing she pass away. So I never did see Memphis Minnie no more.

Son Bonds and I used to play together. He was a good guitar picker. Somebody killed him in Dyersburg, Tennessee, not too far from Ripley. He was settin' on the porch; went to sleep and somebody killed him. I don't know who. He was at somebody's house in Dyersburg. I guess he had been drinkin' some.

I played with Homesick James Williamson a lot.[1] He'd come to my house and learn a lot of stuff to play. Yeah, he a good player; plays guitar. He's still living. He overseas all the time. He is in California right now. This man wants me and him and Henry Townsend go to California to make some record in July, a blues festival. Called me last year and I wouldn't go. He wants four of us, Robert Lockwood too. Homesick and I never did make no record together.

Now, Big Joe Williams and I made some record together, with Sonny Boy too. Big Joe was a big jealous musician. Play a nine-string guitar. Had an extra key put on it. That the way he play guitar. He put out "Baby Please Don't Go." Him and Sonny Boy put that 'un out together. Yeah, he was the jealousest musician in the world, because he get mad if I play a piece and someone else say, "I like the way you play a piece," and don't tell him. He ready to fight. Yeah! We go to play somewhere and another band gonna play, he'll leave. Go way out so he can't hear it. That's the way he done it. Me and him got to fightin' one night in a man's house. I played boogie woogie and he played boogie woogie. But I was playin' guitar then.

Man say, "Yank, you can play some boogie woogie. Play it again."

Big Joe go, "What you want to say that for? He can't beat me playin'! He can't beat me!"

"Yeah, but I want to hear him."

He got mad and left. He do that all the time.

John Henry Barbee was from around Ripley. He played guitar by hisself. I played some with him. Didn't go out nowhere else, no gig or nothin'. I'd

---

[1] Homesick James Williamson is from Somerville, Tennessee, near Rachell's hometown of Brownsville.

run up on 'em; we'd play some together. "Well, you could be sweet, but you don't be sweet no more. Every time I come to your house, a man standin' in your door." Old Barbee, he could sing and play good. Yeah, that one of his songs.

Now you talk about some guitar man, no one could beat Sharron Hayley. He a guitar man! I never got anything over on him! Jess Rawls could play pretty good too, but that Sharron Hayley took 'em all down. He from Brownsville. Yeah, he lived out in the country, he did. They said Son Goss was better than Sharron Hayley. I never did meet Son Goss, but that Sharron Hayley, I knowed what he was. I set and look at him many times play. There was a whole bunch of good musicianers from around there. They never made any records. Me and Sleepy John first black boy made some record. Me and John the first ones down there.

I used to play with Jess Rawls. He was the best guitar man till Willie Newbern come through there. Willie Newbern shut 'em all down, all down but Sharron Hayley; couldn't handle him! Jess Rawls. And he had a son come up play with me too. I went with his daughter, Annie Mae. I was engaged to marry her, but I didn't. I married Ella Mae 'stead of Annie Mae. But he didn't get mad. Naw.

I used to play with Walter Franklin. And Willie Newbern and Stoke Franklin used to play together; them suckers was bad. Walter Franklin left Brownsville, went to Humboldt and he ate something that killed him. Walter played guitar. His brother Stoke played bass. Willie Newbern played mandolin. They had a good band together; the three were good. I learnt some from them, "Texas Tony" and a lot of other pieces that I learned from them. Yeah.

Well, a lot a them guys they didn't play the style of blues I play now, 'cause I play down-home blues. They could play, but they weren't playin' no blues all the time. They were playin' this sentimental stuff, ballads, country music. But I play the blues. They wadn't playin' what I play. Like Sharron Hayley and all of 'em, they were playin' all that kind of stuff. And Jim Jackson, he was from Nashville, a guitar player.[2] He play "John Henry was a steel drivin' man," all that kind of stuff, Elizabeth Cotton and all that. I played with him some. And B. Johnson, he's a boy live in Jackson.[3] He play the violin and he play with us once or twice. I never did record with him, but we did play together. It sound good though. Violin, mandolin, guitar, and harmonica. Man, we made some pretty music.

He stayed around Jackson. We didn't go out nowhere together. I didn't like the fiddle too much and so I didn't fool with carryin' him. I think he was married, anyway. But he didn't know too much about no blues or nothin' like I did, and I didn't fool with him.

But come down to the down-home, old blues that what I play. I used to play that kind of stuff too, like waltzes, but I like the blues the best. I don't play that sentimental stuff no more. I play the blues. That's what come to my mind.

HAMMIE NIXON

Hammie Nixon started playing under me and Sleepy John. I'd play the mandolin; he'd make a note on his harp. I'd make a note for him, for him to find it on the harmonica. So I teach him how to play the harmonica, so he play with me and Sleepy John for a while. But after I cut loose from him, him and John went together. But me and John used to play together all the time.

But I got married and commenced having children. I couldn't run around like John. Well, John pick up Hammie. Anybody can play something, so John carry him with him. I couldn't do that traveling, so I went to Jackson and met Sonny Boy.

Hammie was a nice fellow, a good harp blower too. We used to go together. Hammie, he a pretty smart guy. He hung around Chicago a lot and got one or two of his fingers cut off some kind of way. But he got money out of that. I don't know if he aimed to get his fingers cut off or not, but he got paid for it.

---

[2] Rachell is possibly referring to the Jim Jackson who was born in Hernando, Mississippi, and was based in Memphis. Born in 1890, he played with Gus Cannon's jug band and had a lifelong participation in traveling minstrel shows. He made some recordings on Vocalion and Victor between 1927 and 1930.

[3] Rachell did record with a violinist named Charlie Johnson in New York in 1934. Johnson evidently was from Jackson, Tennessee, as they recorded as the Jackson Shieks.

So he got a job and kept an old car, an old Plymouth. He'd ride around and drink, have a good time. Guy passed us one day had a new car, and he had plenty girls with 'im. Hammie drive an old Plymouth. He dip snuff; had snuff all over the side of it, you know. They passed by laughing at us, "Tehehehe!" you know. He say, "I'm gonna fix 'em." He wound up that raggedy old car and passed 'em. And when he got there, the man done say, "Man, what kind of motor that you got in there?"

He said, "A car motor. What kind of motor you got in your car? You got a new car." That old car outrun the man and he feel so bad. Hammie kept that old car around.

And we play a few places. Humboldt, we play over there about every night, Humboldt, Tennessee. He come back to Brownsville and get me and we play there, and Jackson. Me and Hammie play together a long time. Sometime we didn't know where John Estes was. He be in Chicago, anywhere with somebody.

Once, way back, me and Hammie Nixon went to Mississippi. We travelin' together. I told 'em I was Muddy Waters. Hammie said he was Little Walter. We went there and played. Man! We mopped up pretty good! They thought I was Muddy Waters and Hammie was Little Walter. Hammie was blowin' the harp. I'm playin' the guitar. Made plenty of money! I told them anything, but nothin' bad. But I was just gettin' by. They didn't know what Muddy Waters or Little Walter look like. We was lucky. They just heard the name.[4]

'Nother time me and Hammie and John were playin' in some city. John drink and Hammie drink. So John was blind and they'd go get a fifth of whiskey and they drink it. Hammie try to drink it all. Hand John the bottle. John couldn't see, but he'd shake it. John say, "That son of a bitch done drunk up all this whiskey."

I say, "No, he ain't." See, I was the boss over the drinkin', you know.

I set there; I said, "Hammie, you a fool. You settin' here and some man in your house in Brownsville lookin' at your TV, and you here tryin' to play music." I was jokin' with the fool. Sure enough, the fool got up and left the

---

[4] Rachell and Nixon's impersonation act was most likely done in the early 1950s when Muddy Waters and Little Walter had hit songs on the radio and jukeboxes.

next day. But we were playin' for the man, had to play a week for him. And that was the middle of the week. And he got up and left John and me there. John blind, had a guitar and suitcase. I had a mandolin and suitcase. He go an' left us up there. He got that bus and left the next day. And I said, "I just jokin' with the fool. I didn't know it sure enough." He was drunk. Me and John had to finish playin' out them three days. We laughed about it later when I saw Hammie.

MARRIED

I got married in September 1937. I quit goin' with John different places. Then he took Hammie up with the harp, you see. Hammie wadn't married, you know. Well, I had a wife; I couldn't go followin' him all the time.[5] So he pick Hammie up and let Hammie go play with him two, three years. I couldn't go, but John wouldn't, never would work. But I had to work. I had children and John and Hammie would go, but I wouldn't go.

I married a preacher's daughter. Ella Mae was my wife's name. She been gone thirty years now. Had four children, two boys, two girls. Jess, he was born in Brownsville. Willa B. was born in Brownsville, Maenell was born in Brownsville, and James Jr. was born in Brownsville.

My oldest son and Maenell went to school with Tina Turner. She had a sister. She had a uncle who was a bootlegger; he moved to Brownsville. Tina Turner was from Nutbush. She went back home, I think, last year. They had a big write-up on it.

All my grandkids were born here in Indianapolis. My two girls livin'. Two boys passed away. My last boy just pass away in May. He was a gospel singer. All of 'em sung gospel songs. Still goin' on; they got a gospel group with my granddaughter. She play bass for them and sing too. Two granddaughters sing.

And that son of mine, he got this town sewn up singin' gospel songs. He had the beautifulest wake ever been in Indianapolis, in May 1996. Big J. C.

---

[5] Estes and Nixon recorded August 2–3, 1937, in New York. Apparently, Rachell was planning to get married and didn't want to look like he was running out.

was the name. They traveled everywhere. He had both legs off from diabetes. They go Chicago, New York, Detroit, somewhere, every week. He went in a wheelchair; put the chair in the back of the car and carry him. He were a big songster, best songster in this city.

My wife's father was a preacher, Wardell Johnson. He was a good preacher. We had a band to play in his church. I play mandolin and another boy play guitar with me. Play church songs. The Gospel String Band, that's what my father-in-law named it. He had some daughters. My wife and her sisters, well, they sung there with their daddy, you know. And I played mandolin and my wife was a good songster. She was a big church woman, and so I'd go and sit down and play for 'em till midnight. They say, "Oh, that sure is nice." Well, he didn't say nothin' to me, and I'd go out and play the blues.

My father-in-law had a church in Jackson and one just outside of Brownsville, and he had a church up here in Indianapolis, too. We'd come up here and sing sometimes. I forget the name of it.

I play gospel songs in all his churches and then I get off and go to a house party and play the blues and drink that white whiskey. Yeah. But I wouldn't let him know what I was doin', you know. But he know I'm drinkin' and all.

Chapter 10

Sonny Boy, he'd ride around Jackson on a bike. Me and Dan Smith were playin' together then. Jackson not too far from Brownsville and we'd play there some. So Sonny Boy wanted to play with us, but we didn't pay him no attention.

In 1934 I recorded in New York with Dan Smith. Sonny Boy wanted to go, but he was just a boy ridin' a bike in Jackson. I didn't carry him 'cause I didn't think he was good enough to go, which he was. I found out after I got back.

Cab Calloway's sister was in the hotel we was stayin' at in New York.[1] I don't know the name of the hotel. We got a fifth of some kind of whiskey, twenty-five cent a quart. Two pay a dime and the other one pay a nickel. The one pay a nickel went to get it and brought it back. I don't know what kind of whiskey it was, but we drinked it.

Dan Smith was all right. He was a good guitar player, and he come back from New York, he had some rubber money. I was back in Brownsville and he was in Jackson. He went to a nightclub in Jackson upstairs, and he was pullin' out that rubber money. He come from New York and people thought it was good money, and they killed him. Robbed him to take it, and they didn't get nothin' but some rubber money. He flashin' it and he hadn't made that kind of money in New York and people thought he made a lot of money there. He walkin' around, you know. He hadn't been nowhere. But them guys watchin' him and saw he had some money. They money hungry. When he come down the stair somebody killed him. Didn't get nothin' but all the fishy money. Yeah, the way I heard it.

So after I came back from New York I got to playin' with Sonny Boy. And me and him and John got together and played some. I went out to play with Sonny Boy one night. Went to a man house, went playin' there. Man's wife got stuck on him. Run us all away from there; we left. So after Sonny Boy and I started playin' together, I found out he could play. So then me and him went to making records.

He used to ride a bike around Jackson, and I was working on the dairy farm. He used to come out to the dairy farm. The straw boss out there loved for him to come out there. He loved milk; the man give him all the milk he could drink and he would blow the harp for 'em. The straw boss and his family liked it. Yeah, Sonny Boy, he would sing and blow a harp too.

Then I started playin' with Sonny Boy, and John and Hammie were playin' together. Me and Sonny Boy played together a long time, but me and John would go back to playin' together. We never did quit playin' together. But when he wadn't 'round I played with Sonny Boy, 'cause John didn't stay in

---

[1] Blanche Calloway was a well-known blues and jazz singer at the time about which Rachell is talking.

one place. He here today and tomorrow he may be in Chicago, or anywhere. But I couldn't do that. I was workin'.

I was livin' in Brownsville, and Sonny Boy was livin' in Jackson, twenty-five miles from Brownsville. He catch the bus and come to Brownsville. Stay two or three nights, and the next time I catch the bus to Jackson and stay with him two or three nights.

Oh, Sonny Boy was a good songster! He could play that harp too! He went to Chicago and started a lot of 'em playin' right now. They playin' Sonny Boy's stuff. A lot of songs me and Sonny Boy made, he went to Chicago and play it, and them guys up there playin' it right now. Yessir!

Sonny Boy always gettin' into trouble over women. There's one time I carried him out of a club we were playin'. He tried to court a man's wife, and the man wanted to kill him. He young, you know. He hadn't been out. He didn't care nothin' 'bout that. Yeah, he'd hug 'em and kiss 'em anyway. Keep playin', and would fight 'cause he wasn't scared of nobody. He was a friendly fellow. Kept a smile on him all the time, but he loved that whiskey.

Yeah, I and Sonny Boy travel some. Travel most far with Sleepy John than I did with Sonny Boy, 'cause me and Sleepy John went overseas. But me and Sonny Boy played around Brownsville. We didn't play around much in the country like I and Sleepy John did, because I knew John 'fore I did Sonny Boy, and John was older than Sonny Boy. But after Sonny Boy got 'quainted with me, so we did a lot of recordin' together for Lester Melrose.

They was good friends, John and Sonny Boy. They were different kinds of people, but I got along with all of 'em. They knowed me and I knowed them. So, I knowed Sonny Boy way; I knowed Sleepy John way. Sonny Boy all right. You get too much whiskey in him, he'd act up sometime. But we never had no trouble. I and him didn't.

I and John, we'd make like we gonna fight all the time. Be in the car goin' somewhere to play, we start to arguing. Tell the man, "Stop the car! Stop the car!" I get out on one side; he get out on the other 'un. We get out, but we wouldn't fight. Get out, all go on laughing, and then come back. Well, there were a lot of ups and downs. I can't think of everything now, you know. It's been a long time, a long time.

Chapter 11

At the time I played a lot with Sonny Boy, I used to work for a man on a dairy farm. He had a lot of cows. I milked cows twice a day, morning and night. And when he had a lot of hay to bale, hell, hay baling! Settin' in the fields in September, hottest day in the world, he'd bring a load of hay there. Put it there for you to bale hay, bale that hay. I didn't care. This was when I was grown, workin' on the dairy farm.

I made a record about it, "J. L. Dairy Blues." When I was workin' for him I went to New York and made a record about his dairy farm, Robert Thornton. "I got four cows to milk, have to milk them twice a day."

Yeah, I milked cows, four cow a day, twice a day, mornin' and night. Get up five o'clock and get them cows. *Thumb! Thumb! Thumb! Thumb!* The milk go in the old pail. Old cows, some of them ya had to put kickers on their foot. Keep 'em from kickin' your milk over. Sometime they still kick over the milk. I get so mad I'd whup 'em. And I go in there, the milk house, and bottle up the milk. Quart bottle. Had a thing the milk come in; you pour the milk in that quart bottle and put a stopper on it. I had to bottle it up; put it in a case. Then the boss man, supervisor, I mean, the little old man over us, you know, he'd take it and carry it to town. Sell the milk.

He drinked all the time. So, I had a brother-in-law was a bootlegger. The boy live here in Indianapolis now. When me and my wife come up here he was here. He was married to my wife's sister; his name John Moore. But he was a bootlegger down there. And this man would carry milk, Sol Askew; he work for my big boss man, Robert Thornton. But he drinked all the time. Man get in the truck, carry the milk to town, and he sell it. He said, "Yank, go by John, get us a pint." He sellin' that old, bonded liquor, you know. "Go by and get us a pint." I go by and get it. He drink; me and him drink some. But the big boss didn't know he drink, you know. But he's drinkin' all that money up. Drunk that money up.

So this brother-in-law here now, John Moore, he was workin' for a white man named Arthur Pitman, at a garage. So in Covington, Tennessee, thirty mile from Brownsville, we were goin' out there and get this whiskey. They got so much whiskey the boy was hidin' it under the hood of his car. So one night I went with him get some whiskey. Them police watch you down there.

See, we was bringin' it back to Brownsville. I had half a pint of gin. I just drinkin' it. I looked back. He said, "That's the police!"

I said, "Sure is!" Uh! I throw the bottle out. Police drove up there.

He said, "What you drinkin'?"

I said, "Nothin'."

"You ain't got no whiskey?"

I said, "No."

He searched the car. If he had a raise the hood, he'd a found all the whiskey in there of the boy who bring it back to Brownsville to bootleg it.

So he workin' for the white man and didn't nobody bother him. The police wouldn't come down there foolin' with him. But he bootleg a long time, and so he had some whiskey. He had it hid. Me and Mr. Saul Askew go into town sellin' milk. Come on back. "Get us a pint." Well, I know where my brother-in-law had it hid at. I go get a pint, bring it up, and we get in the truck and come on and drink it up! Next day, milk them cows, I bottle the milk up. Oh, about twenty cases of milk. We sold the milk. We'll get some more whiskey. Drink a pint a day, he would. And I help him drink it.

There was a Shorty Smith. He's a little ol' deputy police, little ol' country police. He was always hangin' out near us. We go out in the county play music. At night he slip out there, to catch us sellin' white whiskey. It was a dry county, you know, Haywood County. He'd try to catch you sellin' whiskey and put you in jail, something like that. Shorty Smith, that was all he good for, crawlin' under the house tryin' to catch ya.

One night I was drinkin' some and he come on out. I throwed the bottle away. He couldn't do nothin' about that. If he'd a caught me with the whiskey, he'd a carried me to jail. I never got caught. Sometime I'd hide the whiskey under my father-in-law's house. I figured the police wouldn't go poking around no preacher's home.

Chapter 12

Nineteen thirty-eight I went to Chicago to record. Lester Melrose used to have Walter Davis come down to the country and pick us up, we music boys, and we'd go and record for him. Him, Sonny Boy, Big Joe Williams, and I would go record together. Walter was a piano player and he was a good musician. And then, after he quit that, he'd taken a hotel in St. Louis and run a hotel for the guy.

One time I was in a car with Sonny Boy and Walter Davis. Big Joe Williams was drivin', and Sonny Boy and Walter started fightin'. Well, neither one was a scared of the other and both of 'em want to fight. They were good friends, but Walter get mad 'cause Sonny Boy drinks. Sonny Boy drink his whiskey, and they got to arguing about it and drinkin' until they want to stop the car and get out. There's a pistol in the dashboard. It wadn't Joe Williams' pistol. It my pistol, so I got it and put it in my pocket so nobody got hurt, 'cause I know they would hurt one another.

But Walter Davis killed a man once later after then. A fella came after him with a knife one Mother's Day night. Old Walter Davis carried a .45. He killed him and got out of it.[1] And Sonny Boy drink, he wadn't scared of Walter Davis. And I and Joe Williams kept them from fightin' best we could. That's the way that was.

So we went to record in Chicago and early that mornin' police come there, want to arrest us. We told them what we were there for. They let us go on and we made the recordin' and come back. We was sittin' in the car when the police came. See, we got there just before day, and we stayed in the car till day come and we went on to the studio. We slept there in the car. It was in Aurora, Illinois, outside of Chicago.

Everything set up in the recording studio when you get there: piano and everything, two, three fifths of whiskey. Lester Melrose had that, 'cause Sonny

---

[1] A man who thought Davis was after his girlfriend pulled a knife on him in a tavern, and Davis shot him. He got off on self-defense. Henry Townsend describes this incident in detail in his autobiography (*A Blues Life* [University of Illinois Press, Chicago and Urbana, 1999], pp. 75–76).

Boy ain't goin' to play 'less he got him some whiskey. Not play good anyway. So every studio we went to be set up with that while we recorded.

Lester Melrose was a nice fellow. I made a lot of record with him on Bluebird. ".38 Pistol Blues," "Yellow Yam," "Skin and Bones," "Up North Blues," "Down South Blues," "Peachtree Blues," I made all them with him. And he passed away. I got two hundred dollars royalty off it, his wife sent. I didn't get no more of that. But I know I had more up there, but I didn't get no more of it. Well, he treated me all right; I just didn't get no royalty from him before he passed away.

I never wrote a song. Go in the studio, it always come to me just like that. Them words, I'd match 'em up, just come to me. No way I wrote a song. No sir. I reckon it's just in me. You know a lot of people go in the studio with a lot of paper and stuff. I don't do nothin'. Me and Sonny Boy would go in the studio, play what we want to play, name it, and come out. I and John done the same thing. But me and Sonny Boy done it more than John did, 'cause John'd be gone all the time. Didn't stay in one place. He'd carry his guitar.

Well, the record studio was up there on Lake Michigan, and while I was there I recorded a song about it, "Lake Michigan Blues." "So long, deep and wide. I see my baby on the other side. I be so glad when Lake Michigan go dry. I'm standin' here with tear in my eye." I made that up in the recordin' office. "Lake Michigan Blues."

".38 Pistol Blues," another one I recorded there, I wrote that. Me and Sonny Boy did. There a little story about it. I was goin' with a woman and a guy was messin' around with the woman. I said, "I'm gonna get my .38 pistol, 'cause my girl ridin' around in a V-8 Ford. And I heard somebody run out my house, out my back door." Well, she's ridin' with the guy, you know.

There was a little nightclub down the street in Brownsville call Tom Wilson's Place. Tom Wilson's Place a cafe down the hill, a underground cafe, you know. That where all the blacks hung out on that side of the street. On one side was a pool room, next were Mae's place, next were Al Rawls' Place. He the one run the funeral home. He the biggest colored guy, had the biggest funeral home in Brownsville. I said in the song, "I catch my woman down by Tom Wilson again, somebody gone fade away. That's why I carry my .38

pistol every day. And I got a sweet thing. She live down on Lover's Lane. I'm so crazy about that woman, yeah, I'm afraid to call that woman's name."

Yeah, the girl run the restaurant was named Addie Mae. I said, "I had a little trouble just on the other side of Tom Wilson's, right down below Mae's Place." I wrote it that a'way, some kind of way. Been a long time, but I remember some of it. That the ".38 Pistol Blues." I first said .45, but the man said, "Why don't you say .38, and they know what you talkin' about?"

"Well, you see I carry my .45."

But he said, "Why don't you put .38?" Well, I wrote that.

"Peachtree Blues" was another 'un I did for Lester Melrose: "Standin' here, baby, lookin' up your big peachy tree. You say you love me so well, please drop one down to me." I match 'em up that a'way!

I wrote "Insurance Man Blues" 'bout the same time. A guy had insurance business and he ask me to write a song about it, about how his insurance pay off good. I sang about Turkey Slim. Turkey Slim was in his insurance. But Turkey Slim died, you know, and they paid him off. They pay his sister off for Turkey Slim. And so he want me to write the song so the more people would join his insurance 'cause he was so good about payin' off, you know, after he died. Well, I wrote the song best I could: "Turkey Slim, he died in the electric chair, but they paid him anyhow." But I never got paid for that song! I'm supposed to have plenty money and I ain't got a nickel and a nail. This company wanted me to write this song, tell the people they don't care how you die.

"Wadie Green" a song about two sisters. One name Wadie; the other 'un name Mary. "I wanna see my little old Wadie Green. I wanna see my little old Wadie Green, 'cause old Mary, she do tolerable well, but little old Wadie, Wadie, she a burnin' hell." She was pretty.

I wrote "Biscuit-Bakin' Woman" 'bout my wife: "Gon' tell the world about that biscuit-bakin' woman of mine. She ain't tall; she kinda low, but good golly molly, can she roll her dough. She a biscuit-bakin' woman, don't you know. She bake 'em in the morning; she bake 'em at night. You get up in the mornin and they just right. The biscuit-bakin' woman, tell the world about the biscuit-bakin' woman of mine."

And I wrote another song about her: "The worried blues sure make a man feel bad. If these worried blues don't kill me, they will be the worst that I had had." That the "Worried Blues."

She never did say nothin' about it. She didn't like much blues, 'cause her father was a preacher, you know. And she wadn't raised with no blues much. But after I married her she had to hear 'em, 'cause I played 'em. She didn't want me to sing it, but I sung it. She was workin' for a lady. She workin' for a white lady. The lady was name Miss Nell, and she was pretty. She said, "When the baby is born, name her Nell, Maenell." My wife was name Ella Mae. Maenell, that's my baby daughter at the house now. So that when I write that song 'bout the biscuit-bakin' woman, she was cookin', workin' for that lady. Then she said, "Tell him to write a song about how you cook." So she come home, told me about it, so I wrote it. That song did pretty good.

I used to stay at Tampa Red's house in Chicago when I went there to record. Lester Melrose would pay Tampa Red and we'd stay at his house. Tampa Red had a bird. He'd fly over to the tavern, they'd put a note in his mouth, and he'd come back to Tampa Red. Had an old dog in there. You didn't give him a drink of beer, he'd bite ya. That's the truth! You drink some beer and don't give him some, you better get out from there. That sucker eat you up! People think that's a lie! But it's the truth! We would get our food out, go to a cafe and eat.

Tampa Red played a lot of slide. I don't care much about no slide player. I didn't play slide, nor Sleepy John. I knew how to play it, but I didn't use it on no record 'cause I don't like slide that much. Some of 'em crazy about bottleneck music, but I don't care for it. But Tampa Red played a lot of that. He was a nice fellow. We got on.

Lester Melrose gave me a guitar one time. It had belong one time to Big Bill Broonzy, but Lester Melrose had it. See, Sonny Boy wanted a briefcase. He wanted a briefcase so bad and Lester gave him a briefcase. He gave me the guitar; I didn't want no briefcase, so he give me the guitar. He made me a present of it, 'cause he gave something to Sonny Boy. It was a nice guitar too. And I brought it to Brownsville. I thought I'd go to Memphis, and my wife told me, "Don't carry it down there." But I went to Memphis with the guitar, and there was a whole crowd of people in front of a music store. Two guy was playin' music, you know.

I ask a guy, "Who is that playing?"

He said, "Yank Rachell and Sonny Boy Williamson, two boys out of Mississippi."

I said, "Yank Rachell?" I went and got me a half pint of liquor and drank it and came back there. I say to one of them feller playin' music, "Who you say you is?"

"Yank Rachell."

And I had my card with me. I said, "Now lookie here, now you're going to jail 'cause you ain't no Yank Rachell. I'm Yank Rachell."

He say, "Mister, don't do nothin' with us. We just tryin' to make a livin', make some money."

I said, "Well you better get outa here, or I'll have you put under the jail."

So they left. I got my guitar and come up the street. And a man drivin' a milk truck stop. "Hey! Let me see that guitar."

I give it to him and he take a lick or two.

"What'll you take for it?"

I'm tryin' to bluff him, you know. I said, "Sixty dollars." He give it to me and drove off. Sold that guitar.

My wife said, "See, I told you not to take that guitar." That guitar had diamonds in the neck of it, a real good guitar. I have sold some real good guitar. I'll never do it again. Yeah, that was Big Bill's guitar. Big Bill Broonzey was all right. He was good. I played some with him in Chicago, not in no club, just settin' around someone house.

Chapter 13

One time I played and a woman tell me, "Oh, you sure favor my husband. I'm gonna talk with you."

I was settin' down playin', and I said, "All right." Drinkin' white whiskey. She's a good lookin' woman.

She say, "That's my car settin' there."

I say, "It is?"

"Ain't it, girl?"

She had a girlfriend with her. She say, "Yes it is."

She say, "I'm goin' to take you home with me tonight."

"Oh yeah?"

I play much harder. I'm a fool, young boy. Ain't got no sense. You know women swell your head. Got through playin'. I said, "John, I'm goin' this gal's home."

"Hell, James, what you want to go with her? You don't know nothin' about that woman."

Said, "I'm gonna find out somethin' 'bout her. You want to go?"

"Hell no, I ain't goin'."

I said, "Well, I'm goin' with her."

Got through playin'; got my little music. Got in the car with her, you know. She turned the radio on, down the street playin'. I said to myself, "I'm into somethin'." I said, "Hot dog, I'm gonna call my mama and tell her how I'm doin'." Went on to her house. A country boy ain't been nowhere. Pull up into a big garage. I said, "Damn, I'm into something. A rich woman." Rug that deep in the floor. Hot damn! Went in the bedroom, big old bed with a light on.

I said, "Where your husband?"

"He in the army, honey. He no trouble. I ain't got nobody and you just put me to mind of my husband. You the same size and everything. Come on in."

Half drunk, went on in. Went downstairs. She give me somethin' to drink. Somethin' look like a goose neck. Somethin' come out of it. I don't know somethin' what it was. I take a drink of it. Oh, I felt so good.

She said, "I know you tired."

I said, "I ain't tired."

She said, "You can take a wash up if you want to. Over in the closet there his pajamas. You the same size; it'll fit you." Say, "You can go on out there and take a bath."

I went there and that big white tub. Hell, I wadn't used to that. I took a bath and dried off.

Says, "Come on upstair now."

Went up the stair. That pretty bed, you know, I looked at it. I wanted it too. I was crazy.

So, she said, "You can lay down."

I'm a fool, lay down.

She had a paper, said, "I'm gonna lay down in a minute with you. I always read this strip. You go on and take a nap; go on and lay down. I won't wake you up."

I lay down and went to sleep. After a while something kept a punchin' me in the side. I woke up; there was a great big man standin' over me with a baseball bat and a .45.

He said, "Goddamn what the hell you doin' in the bed with my wife?" He said, "What's he doin' here?"

She said. "I don't know how he got in the bed, honey. I was readin' here. You left the window up."

He said to me, "Well, I'm gonna kill you. You here in my bed." Said, "I bought this bed, man. That's my house here."

And I had my music settin' over there. Had my clothes off in the corner.

He said, "I'm gonna kill you."

She said, "don't kill him in here."

I said to myself, "Now I ought to tell my mama what I'm doin'. I don't need to tell my mama that!" *Thump. Thump! Thump!* My heart's beatin'.

He said, "Get up."

"Honey, don't kill him in here."

"I ain't gonna kill him in here. Pull off my pajamas. He got my pajamas on. Now how he do that?"

"Honey, I don't know."

"Get your clothes and put 'em on."

Well, I'm watchin' 'im so I put my pants on backwards. He made me put 'em on right.

He said, "Get your mandolin. Get your music. I got a radio. I don't need none of your music. Come on the door. You got to head outside. I'm gonna kill you."

I walked a piece and turned around.

He said, "Go ahead."

I got out on the step. I said, "Lord, this man gonna kill me." Then, *Boom!* He hit me. I lit out runnin'. He shot again. *Bamm!* Kept a goin'. I had $180 in my pocket. When I end up, I didn't have a dime. Took my money off me. I said, "Man, that learn me a lesson. From now on I won't do that no more."

Went on again to lady's house. Said, "Yeah, I'm divorced." I went on in there. I didn't have no sense; I was young. Went on to her house. Say, "Yeah, we been married, but I'm divorced now." Went up there, upstairs. Come down. Heard somebody knock on the door.

"Who at my door?"

"What the hell! You know who it is. Open this door!"

Well, I in there.

Say, "If you don't open it, I'm gonna tear it down. Open it." He hit the door pretty hard.

I said, "Mister, don't tear the door down 'cause I'm in here. I got my gun." Say, "I'm gonna kill you 'cause your wife told me that you wadn't married."

He said, "Well goddamn. You wait till I come back."

I said, "Well, I'll be here when you come back."

When he went that a'way, I went this a'way! Man, I come out of there flyin'! I'm tellin' you I been through all that stuff. I don't care what woman, where she at. I ain't goin' with no woman to her house! Naw. Uh uh. Don't you do that, boy. Don't you go with no woman home. They tell you anything. They get to likin' you, some of 'em, tell you anything, and do thing that spite ya up. Uh uh. No. You can go to my house. I ain't goin' to yourn. Uh uh. I ain't gonna do that.

Yeah, one woman tried to get me to jump out of a three-story house one night, you see. There's a lots to know in this world. I met the guy. He a nice fella. Had me to his house; he live upstairs. I went to his house. Me being a dog, I liked the damn wife, you know. She live upstairs and have a grate. She have some ham and fry it on the grate on the fireplace, you know. Had a fireplace upstairs. We eat supper. This guy was a Pullman porter. Well, I know he was goin' out on this route.

He said, "Well I'm goin' on my run. It's time for me to go. My train will be through directly, but you ain't got to hurry." Say, "You can stay here and keep my wife company till you get ready to go."

I said, "No I'm goin' on when you go."

I went with him to make sure he catch the train. He caught the train. I'm goin' back to his house like a fool. Went on upstairs.

She say, "He gone?"

I say, "Yeah, he got that train and gone."

He wadn't gone. He paid somebody to take his run, so after a while he come back home.

She say, "I thought you were gone, honey. I was so lonesome."

He said, "No, I didn't feel good, so I give an old boy ten dollars to take my run tonight." He said, "I'm hungry, too. I wanna eat some more. Cook a little piece of ham."

She says, "No, I ain't gonna make no fire in this house now. It's too hot." Say, "I got a dollar and a half on the dresser." Said, "Go down and get ya somethin' to eat."

He said, "No, I ain't gonna walk down there. I'm tired of walkin'."

Well, the gal first told me to hide under the bed, hear him comin' up the steps. She said, "That walk sound like Johnny. Can you hide under the bed?"

I said, "No, I ain't gonna get under the bed."

She said, "Well, jump out the window."

I said, "Honey, that three story. I can't jump out no window!"

She said, "What you gonna do?"

Said, "I got to do somethin'. Say, I'll tell you what. I'll go up this chimney." I got up on the grate there and went up the chimney.

He come in, sat down, said, "Cook me a little piece of ham on the grate there.

She said, "No, It's too hot. I'm not going to make a fire in here now."

He had an old ax that he chopped up kindlin' with. Said, "I'm so glad my mama learned me how to cook." Say, "I'll fry me a piece of ham myself."

Well, now I'm up the chimney. Holed up there, gettin' some breath. Man put some paper down, put some kindling down there. Set a skillet there. Well, that heat comin' up on me now, and it got so hot up there. The chimney was stopped up 'cause I had the chimney stopped up.

He said, "I should 'a had a chimney sweeper up here. I oughta shoot up there and clean it out."

She said, "No, you don't want to be shootin' up there at this time of night, scarin' folks." She said, "Don't you do that."

"Well, there's smoke comin' down; it's about to stiffen me."

Well, so much smoke got in the house, you know. Said, "Open that door. 'Bout to stiffen me to death."

Well, he turned around and opened the door. Well, he opened the door; I was comin' down the steps. Well, he spied me. I scared him. He run down the steps and I run down behind him. I was smokin'. My feet were hot; bottom of my shoes were burn out. He runnin' down the steps. I scared him. He run down the step and I run down the step. He run that a'way and I run this a'way.

Next day I come by he had a truck. I say, "Hey." I say, "You make a run last night?"

"No man."

I say, "What you doin' with this truck?"

"I'm fixin' to move."

Say, "You gonna move from this good place?"

"Man, yeah. This house is hainted."

I said, "What you mean, it's hainted?"

"You know I went to make a fire to cook me something last night and something come down the chimney. Big as you."

Said, "Sure 'nuff?"

"Yeah, this house is hainted."

Said to myself, "Hell, it was me."[1]

But I went on.

I been through all of that. I ain't lyin', so I just say I'm a lucky man to be livin'. I done many thing, different thing, not nothin' to harm nobody, no trouble or nothin' like that. No more foolin' around like that. I learnt better sense.

---

[1] This story uses the following folktale motifs found in Stith Thompson's *Motif Index of Folk-Literature* (Bloomington: Indiana University Press, 1955): K1521.1, paramour successfully hidden in chimney (vol. 4, p. 403); J1786, man thought to be a devil or ghost (vol. 2, p. 148); K521, K547, escape by frightening would-be captors (vol. 4, p. 312).

But, I'll tell ya, I told a boy, if you think your wife playin' on ya, don't fight her. That make her slick. You go to fightin' 'em, that'll make 'em slick. You never will catch her. Just be pleasant to her, "Lover baby, baby," and that. Then she'll get careless, let you catch her. But if you whup her, uh uh! You messed up. You make her slick. She slick already; she'll get slicker then. Ain't nothin' you can do about it.

Chapter 14

I'll tell ya, back in them days, down South, the people wadn't right. They didn't treat you right. They do or done everything to you down there. Seven o'clock they blow you off the streets. They set up the stores and things. We had to go out in the country and pray until daylight. But, you know, a white lady come by wearin' shorts, you better not look at her. "Nigger, what the hell you doin' lookin' at that white woman?" All that kind of stuff, you know. They do you all kinda way back then in Brownsville, the white people. Colored folks catch hell all the time. They kill ya if they think ya outa line.

A boy workin' for a man run a laundry. He was the head worker, Albert, Albert Williams. We call him Big Williams. So one evening he got off work, went home, eat supper, put on his house shoes and housecoat. So, the boss man come down there. You know if I workin' for you, you won't come down to the house. Boss man don't come down to the house of the one workin' for him. Ain't normal. But the boss man go to Albert house and call him out.

"Come here." He come out.

"Get in the car." He got in the car with him. Four or five cars were parked behind the man with their lights out. He and his boss man — carry him on to the Big Hatchie River. The other cars trail 'em on down there, haul him up in the tree, cut his privates off, his fingers and toes off, put a weight on him, and throw him in the river. That's when I left.

Why they did that? Said it was the nigger tryin' to get up some kind of a meetin' or something, tryin' to get up a little organization or something, you know. They didn't like that.

Well, I don't know, it must have been the KKK that hung the kid by the river. Hung him up, them guys. And one man was in Big Williams's group; he never could straighten up no more. He was in that, Ervin Rawls. And some of 'em had strokes, and all that happen to 'em after they done that boy that a'way. Most of 'em went to New York. Lot of boys in New York right now on account of that in Brownsville, after they hung that boy in that tree. And a white lady live down the way, she heard the boy hollerin', but she didn't have no telephone to call nobody to come help the boy. And so the next day the wife come down, and they ask can she identify the body and she say, "Yeah, that's my husband."

Well that lynchin' bother me.[1] After everyone else was leavin', I left too, for a while. People went to Detroit, Chicago, New York. They still over there. I had to watch my ownself with the white people. My playing music and travelin', the white people all, some of them like it, and some of them didn't. They see you; they want you in the field all the time. They see you with a guitar, say, "Well, that nigger ain't no account. He carry a guitar around." They said it about John, but John didn't pay it no attention 'cause he wadn't goin' to work.

Sometime I go way through the cornfield to keep 'em from seein' me 'cause I didn't want anyone to say that about me, 'cause I worked all the time, you know. At night I played, but they didn't understand. Sometime it'd be day before I get home, but I come 'round to it. I didn't want them to see me much with the guitar 'cause they call you no account. "He ain't no account! He a guitar player!" Some of them appreciate it and some of them didn't. The most of 'em didn't appreciate it.

If they say, "I'll fire you," you'd work real good. But they build John a house there 'fore he died in Brownsville. The white people build him a house. And he went blind. I went down there, and it had been forty years, and the mayor of the town give me a key. Say, "You come here back to Brownsville, I'll build you a house."

---

[1] For an account of the Brownsville lynching, see appendix 5.

Some of the people thought it was the worst thing in the world. They thought it was such a disgrace to have a guitar. John Estes never did work nowhere and he carry a guitar, but he didn't stay around there. He in and out. I had a family, I had to stay there, so that's the way that was. I didn't just take music for my livin'. I worked in the day and play at night. I never did trust music for my living. I always had a job.

Workin' at the J. L. Dairy farm, I had trouble over a damn sixteen-year-old white boy. Oh, he wadn't nothin' but a kid, Pitman. Tommy Morris' son was named Pitman. Well, Tommy Morris was a straw boss out there. The man has a house built out there on the farm and he live in there. See, he was workin' for Robert Thornton, we all was on his farm, but he was an overseer of us, you know.

One day he said, "Well, Pitman sixteen now."

I said, "Yeah."

"He want y'all to say Mister to him."

I said, "I'm older than he is. Why I got to say Mister to him?"

"Well, you know that what the colored folk call 'em, Mister, they get to sixteen."

I said, "Well, I'm grown. He ought to say Mister to me, look like."

"Naw, you have to say Mister to him."

I said, "Well, I ain't goin' to say Mister to him."

He didn't like that a'tall, you know. He turn red. But I meant it! They call me a fool in Brownsville. "That Yank Rachell ain't got a bit a sense. He crazy." I wadn't no fool. But I didn't take too much doggin' off none of 'em! Nobody!

Goin' and callin' a sixteen-year-old boy Mister! That what they wanted you to do down there. Yeah. But now all that stuff out now. I went down there; we went down in May 1996 for me to play at the W. C. Handy festival. It was all different.

It was pretty much different. Forty year make a difference. Mayor told me, "You come back down here, I'll build you a house." They bring somebody to take care a ya. Mayor of the town, I didn't know about him when I left there, but I guess he read about me or somethin'. He was a nice man. Gave me a big key, the key to the city. He got me some nice pictures. They take 'em for me.

I'd like to go back down there. But since I got here, I got lot a friend, you know. I know them. But down there a lot of the friend I knowed, they dead and gone. Ain't nobody down there much! Them that there are new, come from the country there. I don't know 'em. They don't know me much, some of 'em don't, so I don't know what to do. I'm settin' straddle the fence. My daughter don't want to go back down there. And I kinda wanta go back, 'cause livin' is cheaper and everything.

I'll get on one of them tractors and ride them! Ain't no horses and mules no more. I used to get up in the mornin' and hook up them mules and plow all day long, followin' that mule.

Chapter 15

I went to St. Louis. My wife told me, "Yank, you better go," 'cause in them times they gang you, you know. Burn your damn house up or anything; they didn't care.

Said, "You better go, 'cause they tryin' to get you and they get all of us. We don't want to stay around here and get killed."

I said, "Well, I ain't goin' nowhere."

She said, "Yeah. You better go."

So, I went to St. Louis. Stayed there awhile.[1]

I had trouble with a white man, Tom King. A guy had a farm and he had a warder man, name was Tom King. I was goin' with a girl name of Betty Burns. Sweet, pretty girl, nice-lookin' girl. Tom King asked me to talk to the girl fo' him. Colored girl, you know, light skinned, pretty.

---

[1] Rachell went back and forth between St. Louis and Brownsville more than once. It is difficult to know which times were short visits to play music and which were longer stays. The lynching in Brownsville that caused him to leave for a while took place in 1940. Robert Koester, Henry Townsend, and David "Honeyboy" Edwards all mentioned that Rachell worked industrial jobs when he was in St. Louis.

I said, "No sir, I won't talk to her."

Mr. King said, "You have to do that."

Well, I was goin' with the one he liked! He didn't like that. I told him, "No, I won't do that." So then he got a little piqued at me, you know.

I went by his house. His house on the side of the gravel road, a gate openin' into the road. So, I went by in my car. I come back he's out the gate.

He says, "Where you goin'?"

I say, "Well, I'm goin' back to town."

He say, "You drivin' too fast."

I say, "Well, I'm in a hurry." I say, "I'm workin', playin' down there at the fish dock." Say, "My band down there. I have to get back up there."

He say, "Well, I'm goin'. I'm gonna drive thirty miles an hour. You better not pass me afore I get to town."

I said, "I don't know sir. You have to drive a little faster than that." I laughed. I said, "'Cause I'm in a hurry, Mr. King."

So Mr. King set out drivin'. My boss man was Mr. Thornton. I was livin' on a dairy farm. He had bought me a V-8 Ford. And this man had an old Chevrolet. Well, that V-8 Ford was fast when it first come out. We was goin' on, so I got to a place where I could pass him, so I went by him. Gravel flew up all on the side of his car. Before I got up to town I stopped, parked side of the road. He caught up with me.

"Uh huh! Goddammit. I told you not to pass me! I'm gonna whup you!"

You know them old jack you put on the car and wind up? He got in the trunk and got that out. Well, I got out of my car. I was goin' this a'way. He come on. I got out of my car and stood there.

He said "I'm gonna whup you."

I said, "No, you ain't gonna hit me with that iron."

"Yeah, I'm gonna whup you."

I said, "No, you don't. Don't you hit me with that iron. Don't you come no further on me."

Well, he stopped. He said, "When I get to town. I'm gonna tell your boss about you. 'Bout you passin' me."

I said, "Alright." Wadn't but about half mile from town then. I know he gonna try and get me in some trouble when I got to town. So my boss man,

Robert Thornton, he roomin' on the milk dairy farm. Tom King met my boss. My boss ridin' in a car; he whistled at 'em, my boss and his wife in the car. They was big-eyed, nice lookin' white folks.

"Hey, Robert. Why, that nigger a yourn stopped down there. I think he threatened me. I think he had a gun. 'Cause I decided to whup him with this damn iron."

He said, "Well, Mr. King, you don't whup my man with a iron." Said, "What'd he do?"

"I told him not to pass me comin' to town."

He said, "Well, Mr. King, I bought him that car and he work for me and he stay with me, so I'll ask you not to try and whup him with no iron. You wouldn't want nobody whup you with a iron, would you?" That made him mad, you know.

So my boss come on, he said, "Yank? What's the matter with you and Mr. Tom King?"

I say, "Ain't nothin' the matter. He want to whup me with a damn iron."

"You draw a pistol on him?"

I said, "No, I ain't drawed nothin' on him. I told him not to come no further. I meant it."

He said, "Well, he ain't gonna whup you with no iron. You think he gonna whup you, gonna bother you tonight, you come to my house." Said, "He won't come to my house and bother you."

I said, "I don't know, Mr. Robert. I don't know why he want to come and pick at me like that." So, I went on home.

Wife told me, "You ought to go to St. Louis. Go somewhere." So I went to St. Louis, stayed there about a year.

I come back, see that same fella. I goin' down the road walkin'. Car behind me, "Come here!" I went to the car. Said, "I ain't got nothin' 'gainst you, boy. What you want to go off for?"

I said, "Well, I just want to keep out of trouble."

"Oh, I ain't gonna bother you."

I said, "I ain't 'fraid of you, Mr. King, 'cause I ain't gonna let you whup me with no iron, no way."

"I don't blame you."

Well, that settled that. Didn't have no more trouble out of 'im.

Someone put a note on the door of my house, so I left Brownsville again. I don't know who done it, but I left. The note said, "Don't let the sundown catch you here."

Well, I didn't want to go. Wife kept on sayin', "You better go, 'cause they may set the house afire. Run us all off." I didn't want them to burn my house up and kill me and my children, so I left. I went to St. Louis.

I didn't take no stuff off of 'em, those white people. I told 'em what I thought about 'em, you know. They didn't like my attitude. When they wadn't right I would tell 'em they wadn't right. Police or sheriff, I'd tell 'em all. They say I crazy. I wadn't crazy.

But I think that guy, old guy call Charlie Kerr, he wanted that house. That what I think who done that. Old colored boy put that sign up there. But I didn't know who done it.

When I come back, I found out that he done it. My folk had to move out the house. I found out that he wanted the house hisself. So he move in the house. I come back; he's in the house. I never will forget that. Cause me to leave there. I thought the white folks done it.

Chapter 16

I had a good old time in St. Louis. Oh, yeah. Played all the time over in East St. Louis; played several places. Sonny Boy was in Jackson and John in Brownsville. I left them and got my family in St. Louis. I worked for Wagner Company, an electric company at 4400 Plymouth. Yeah, a carload of coal come there. That was my job on a Sunday. I unload that coal, and my day work was done. It took a day's work to unload it, too. Man, I been through it. Worked for a furniture company. I always worked. I never did 'pend on my music to make my livin'. Lot a guys quit playin'.

"Man, if I could play like you, I wouldn't work for nobody."

"No, I'm gettin' me a job."

Come the war, I had a letter to go to my local board in Brownsville. I got it in St. Louis, to go into the army, but they were getting younger ones than me to go. I was in St. Louis when they bombed Pearl Harbor, but I didn't have to go.[1]

I was on the Missouri side more, but I would go over to East St. Louis. There was a river we had to cross, three, four bridges. I'd play on the east side. One night I went over there. Guy called Spoon used to play with me and Sleepy John. Beat spoon and all, 'round your head. *Tap! Tap! Tap!* Actin' like he was cuttin' your hair. Yeah, he could beat spoon and all on his knee. Call him Kid Spoon. We played one night at a place in St. Louis. So we got ready to come out. I had a girl with me, and Spoon went and done all that smart talk to the guy that owned the club. I got in my car and the owner called the police to come lock both of us up. Kept us all night. That Spoon doin' a lot of smart talk to the man, and I hadn't done nothin', but he done that smart talk and all. The man locked us up. I had to stay there. I was so mad. I had a new girl too, and she got away from me.

So I was in St. Louis and didn't have no girlfriend. So, next night I went on again. Drive my car down the street, late. Lady come down the street, you know. I'm by myself, you know. She had on red, high-heel slipper with the seam behind. I park and she come over.

"Hello."

I said, "Hey."

She said, "What's goin' on?"

I said, "Oh, nothin'. I'm just catchin' a little air."

"Why can't I catch some air?"

I said, "Sure." Now I don't know her. She's pretty. She got in the car with me.

I say, "What you drink?"

She say, "Scotch."

I went and bought a pint of scotch. Have a big time with her.

---

[1] According to Robert Koester, Rachell worked in a defense-related industry in St. Louis during World War II.

She say, "let's go up on Grand and drink."
I say, "I got a 'partment."
She say, "That's fine. Let's go there."
We goes on to the apartment, you know. I say, "What you eatin'?"
She say, "Shrimp."

I bought some shrimp, carry it on there, and I set there, and set there. After a while she come in and undressin' you know. Well, she had a wig on. I thought it was a woman.

A damn man! I set there. Kept a lookin'. What made me so mad, I kissed her suckin' tongue, and it was a man.

He said, "I'm just like a lady."

I said "Mister, you don't get outta here, I'll kill you." I say, "You done drunk my whiskey, et my shrimp. See, you know you ain't no woman."

"Yeah, I'm just as good as a woman."

I say, "Well, you get out, I can't handle you."

Boy that thing got away with me so bad. So now I'm particular about what I pick up. Everything look like a woman ain't a woman. I'm tellin' you man! Them suckers look all kind of way. Old punk! And I thought I had something goin' for myself.

Peetie Wheatstraw, he used to live in St. Louis. I went to his house. Me and Sonny Boy went to Peetie Wheatstraw's house and met him. His singing and playing something different than anybody else. He had a whoop in his songs: Heeheeyeehaw! A whoop. Nobody sing like him. He call himself the Devil's Son-in-Law and the High Sheriff from Hell. Some preacher said the blues is the devil's music, but I don't think so.

I met Henry Townsend in St. Louis. Henry Townsend a good piano player. I went to his home in St. Louis; I met him back when Sonny Boy was playin'. Henry Townsend used to play some with Sonny Boy. I think Henry's from some part of Mississippi, I reckon. I made some record with him, not that far back, but since Sonny Boy been dead, in the fifties or something like that.[2] We made some record together, and then he want to make some more.

---

[2] Rachell played on three tracks of Henry Townsend's LP *Mule*, which was recorded in St. Louis in 1979 (Nighthawk LP 201).

He called me about it, but I couldn't go right then. So some fellow there wants him to record some. And then he called me this year; want me to go somewhere.

But Henry Townsend want me to go to California with him, about four, five months ago. After the wife died, nobody go with him. See, he along my age, he about a year older than I am. And so he say, "I ain't got nobody to go with me and you ain't got nobody with you." Say, "Can't we make that play? I don't want to go by myself."

Yeah, Henry Townsend a good player. And Robert Junior Lockwood, we all play together. Well, a man call me in California. He want Robert Junior Lockwood, Homesick James, and me and Henry Townsend to come to California. Three thousand dollar and your expenses. Well, I wouldn't go. I'm on that machine, that dialysis, you know, and I wouldn't fool with trying to go down there. California too much for me, anyhow. I don't like California. I don't like no flyin' too much, but me and Sheena, my granddaughter, we flew there and flew back, few years ago.

Robert Junior Lockwood, we used to play some together. He's a good player. He lives in Cleveland now. When I was livin' in St. Louis, I had a guitar there, and Robert Junior was livin' there too. Well, I was playin' and so he just came by the house one day and I didn't know he could play. And a friend of mine, name James McCain, he was always hangin' around me. So he met this Robert Junior, told him, "I know a guy name Yank play the guitar."

Say, "You do?"

"Yeah, he play boogie woogie."

Well, I playin' boogie woogie, so he brought this Robert Junior over there. That's when I met him. He played boogie woogie. Well, Junior didn't have a guitar, but he'd come by and borrow my guitar and go out to the pool room and play for them guys. And so we got to playing together. We went to Newport and play over the river and come back. I've been playing with him ever since.

About three years, four years ago, he had a little blues festival of his own, so I go up there to it and played some for him in Cleveland. And then he come down here once and played in Indianapolis for a girl name Mary Gilmore; she had a big place here. So I ain't see him since.

When I was in St. Louis I used to play guitar. I play so much guitar, man, I thought I knowed too much about guitar. My style, I was playin'. I got a lot of record playin' guitar with different ones, but I can't keep up with 'em.

I knowed Charlie Pickett down in St. Louis too. He got drunk and fell down the stairs. Little old light-skinned guy, big eyes, but he could play pretty good. He played guitar. "Highway 61," he could play and sing it too, that was his song. He was from down about Ripley, Tennessee. We played gigs together in St. Louis. Play some in East St. Louis, some of them bars. A long time ago but I can remember it, you know.

I first met Jimmy Walker in St. Louis. We been good friends ever since. A real piano man, Jimmy Walker. He older'n me. We used to play at some club; you go down in the basement. Yeah, we play with Sunnyland Slim and St. Louis Jimmy. Sometime Sleepy John come down to play with us.

Chapter 17

Sonny Boy tried to get me to go to Chicago two or three times. Sonny Boy had come from Chicago twice askin' me to go up there with him. He first went to St. Louis, Sonny Boy did. He had an uncle live in St. Louis. Well, I went with him to St. Louis. We stayed up there and played round, and we come back to Jackson. Well, he go to Chicago. Come back. He say, "Yank."

I say, "What?"

"Man, let us go to Chicago. We'll make plenty money up there."

I said, "I can't go, man. I got a wife and children."

"Well, carry 'em with you! You know there's plenty money."

I said, "No, I can't go up now."

So he went to Chicago. 'Bout a month he come back. "Man, we need you! We need you in Chicago! Come on, let's go!"

I said, "I can't go, Sonny Boy. I'm tellin' you the truth." I say, "I'm up here now makin' a crop. I can't leave it." I say, "Half a crop over there may come up."

So he went back. Next news I heard, they done killed him. That was back in 1948.

Sonny Boy was all right, but he wadn't scared of nobody. I think he playin' at a nightclub in Chicago, and he got to gamblin', and I think he win a lot of money. Had a diamond ring. So he got the money and he half drunk. You didn't tell him nothin'. He get him a cab to go home. Two more guys were watchin' him. They go the same cab, you know. Cab come up, they get in the cab, too. Sonny Boy get off; they got off. That where they knocked him down, jumped on his chest, took his ring and his money, and left. He staggered up to the door and ring the doorbell. Said, "Lacey," that his wife name, "open the door." Said, "I made more money today than I ever made in my life." So she come. He said, "I'm sick. I'm hurt." Called the ambulance; he died before they got to the hospital. That the way I heard it. Yeah.

So I said, "Well, I didn't go with Sonny Boy to Chicago and I'm glad I didn't." 'Cause he drinks too heavy. He get to playin'; he get to drinkin'. That was Sleepy John's trouble too. He drink.

I would drink some, but I never would get too much. I used wouldn't play nothin' lessen I had a drink. But I'd feel, you know, make me feel like playin'. But you get too much, you think you playin' and you ain't doin' nothin' but messin' up. I had to quit that stuff, so I don't drink none now. Ain't had a drink in about ten year now, I reckon. I'm on that medical care. I can't drink nohow and take that medicine. It'll kill ya.

So, I get to thinkin' a long time. I just thank the Lord for me bein' here, 'cause I been through a lot. Lot I know, I can't think of. A lot I know I wouldn't go through with it again, you know. So, I'm eighty-six years old. I'm still livin', thank the Lord. And I still can play a little bit, not like I used ta. I don't care about like I used ta, but I do it now just 'cause I have to make some kind of livin'. They don't have to give me no job 'cause my health bad. I can't work nowhere, and they don't give me no job, so I play me a little music, make me a little money now and then. Doin' the best I can.

My father-in-law, the one told me Sonny Boy was dead, he had a church in Jackson, Tennessee. That's where Sonny Boy live. But I was in Brownsville, but he come home and told me. Said, "Yank, come over." Said, "Heard Sonny Boy got killed."

I said, "You did?"

"Yeah."

I didn't want to hear it no how. I said, "The preacher didn't know what he talkin' about," you know. I didn't believe it. Sure enough, it was true. He told me the truth 'bout it. But he was goin' to Jackson. He kind of courtin' over there, too. I know it, but I wouldn't tell his wife about it.

So he told me about it. "Sonny Boy got killed." Well, he know Sonny Boy 'cause Sonny Boy come over to my house and stay, and I go to Jackson sometime and stay.

They had Sonny Boy's funeral in Jackson. I had to go get the bus to go over there, and I had to wait. But the bus got there too late for me; they had the funeral and gone to the cemetery. I didn't get to see him. Me and my wife caught the bus and went over there, but it was gone. Well, I didn't have my own way to go then, you know, waitin' for the bus.

Chapter 18

Well, my wife had a sister, and the sister and her husband live in Indianapolis. So my wife's mother and father passed.

She said, "Why don't we go to Indianapolis? Mama and Papa dead. Why we stayin' here?"

I said, "I don't know, but how you know you would like it there?"

She said, "I don't know. You want to go see?"

I go up on a bus, stay four days, come back, and say, "Yeah, I like it." I said, "Well, what we goin' do with our house?"

"Rent it out?"

I say, "We ain't goin' get paid for it and they goin' tear it up, so let's sell it."

Sold our house and I hired a big truck to move us up here to Indianapolis. So there was some sanctified people there in Brownsville, church people. I sold my music to the sanctified people. Quit playin'. Said she wanted me to be at home. Didn't want me to be on the road, her and the children, you know. I came up here; been here ever since. That was about 1956.

When I first came to Indianapolis, I got a job driving for Goldstein. He had a furniture store and I drove a truck making deliveries. Then work as a custodian. I retired twenty years ago from Randsburg on Fifty-sixth Street, last place I work.

I thought it was all right here. Wadn't much difference between the people there and here. People about the same here and there. I come here in '56 and my wife die in '61. So she pass away. I never did leave. Still down here, hangin' around with my family. My two daughters livin'. I'm with them now, livin' with my daughter Maenell. A lot of guys begged me to leave.

"Come on, let's go."

I wouldn't do that. Well, I stayed with my children. I'm with my baby daughter right now and my granddaughter. I'm with them; we bought a house. My baby daughter married. Her husband pass away about three years ago. Me and him were buyin' a home together, he pass away, so all the load fell on me. Well, I move in with my granddaughter for a while. She was in an apartment. I stayed there about a month, and I'm lookin' for a house, so I found a house. I bought another house. That record I made, "She Caught the Katie," paid me off. I made a record with Taj Mahal.

When I came to Indianapolis, Shirley Griffith the first guy I met. He come to my house. I thought he was a preacher. He all dressed up. I talk with him. He heard about I come here, so me and him team up together and play, and another guy named J. T. Adams.

J. T. and Shirley played guitar. When I met Shirley Griffith, him and J. T. Adams were playing together. So, me and him and Shirley Griffith played together. Shirley died; he had a heart attack. And J. T. Adams had sugar. He went to get operated on by it, and he died on the table, yeah.

Shirley was a pretty good guitar player. But he couldn't play like J. T. Adams. He was a good player. J. T. didn't make no record, but we played together.[1]

Shirley didn't have too many friends, in a way, but I liked him. He was a nice fella. He was kind of a separate fellow. A lot of 'em didn't like Shirley. There weren't too many people at his funeral. He had a good job workin' at Chevrolet. Had a home, three or four guitars, and he wouldn't be bothered with nobody. He didn't associate much with other people, nobody but musicians. He liked musicians.

Yeah, I take him to Jackson, Mississippi, once. He say he goin' to see his people. That's where his home was, Jackson, Mississippi. So he asked me to go with him down home. I went with him, drove his car. He had an old two-tone Buick. I didn't have a driver license; went all the way through Memphis and come back. He asleep half the time.

Said, "Don't drive the old car too fast."

I said, "I won't."

And he'd go to sleep and I let the blade down on that sucker. We went there and come back. Shirley was a good fellow. I liked him all right, but he wanted to be a big shot.

Well I and J. T. Adams traveled home after Shirley died. I'm the first one put him on the airplane. Got on the airplane. They say, "You all fasten your seat belt," and the airplane hit a pocket and shook it, you know. The glass is rattling. He said, "Woman told me I ought to fasten my seat belt. Well, I'm gonna unfasten it 'cause I done shit!" He commenced to buy those little bottles of whiskey. That tickled me to death. I flied five times overseas and ten times over the water.

Me and Shirley and them played a lot around. We played for parties of all kinds. We didn't go to no nightclubs or nothin'. We go to different houses and set down and play. People have a little picnic out in the yard.

Pete Franklin 'nother guitar player I knowed in Indianapolis. He got all his playin' from Scrapper Blackwell and that boy who play with Scrapper,

---

[1] J. T. Adams and Shirley Griffith recorded an album for Prestige-Bluesville in Indianapolis in 1961 (*Indiana Avenue Blues*, Bluesville 1077).

Leroy Carr. Yeah, Pete Franklin played all that stuff, piano and guitar, anything. But he drunk so much wine that it killed him. "He went down to Clifton, get some alcohol. Told 'em to cover it with water, didn't put in a drop at all. Ooh, this alcohol is killin' him." That one of his songs.

Lefty Bates, we played together, but he died 'bout ten years ago. He wore a hairpiece all the time. We played about the same kind of blues. Shirley Griffith was about the same too. Yeah, a long time ago, long time.

Chapter 19

And so, well, I didn't know what to do after my wife passed away. I was at a loss, lonesome, sad. So John and them called me. Wrote me a letter, would I like to make some record, and I answer and say, "Yeah! I would." So they come up here and got me, and I went to Chicago. We record for Bob Koester, and then, year or two later, he send us to Europe, about ten of us, Sippie Wallace, Little Brother Montgomery, Big Joe Turner, Freddy Below, and this other boy play guitar.

I made a record for Bob Koester, Delmark, called *Mandolin Blues*. It was the first record I made for him and the first record I made in many a year. It was in 1962 or 1963, somewhere in there. Then I cut some more records for him. It didn't take long to make *Mandolin Blues*. We just went up there and made it 'cause, see, Mike Bloomfield and we all used to play around, you know. Then we got ready to record and we already knowed what to do. We just went on up there and made it.

We play a lot o' my songs. "Get Your Morning Exercise," "Lonesome Blues," "Doorbell Blues," my songs. "Move Your Hand," that Big Joe Williams' song.[1] It go, "Move your hand off that rusty can."

---

[1] "Move Your Hand" was composed by Joe McCoy, who recorded it with his Harlem Hamfats on August 14, 1936 (Decca De7218).

"Stop Knockin' on My Door," that's mine, you know. It's about, well, I got a woman in the room; don't knock on the door! "Up and Down the Line," that's mine. I didn't get no royalties on that. I didn't understand how to get nothin', you know. I should have, but they took advantage of me.

Pete Crawford made that *Chicago Style* album with me.[2] I recorded with Bob Koester twice, with Sleepy John, Big Joe Williams, and Mike Bloomfield, and then the next one with Pete Crawford. He play guitar, play it pretty good. And he was playin' with Jimmy Walker in Chicago in some clubs around there. Sometime he and Jimmy would come down here to Indianapolis. They'd even bring Jimmy's piano; load it in a truck and drive on over here. We'd play all week. Drink that whiskey. Tear the house down!

Charlie Musselwhite used to sell record for the Delmark man, Bob Koester. He have a big record store in Chicago, and Charlie would hear our record and things. That where he learned to play the blues, and that where I first met him. He was just a kid and I help bring him up. Used to he couldn't play nothin'.

So out in California three years ago I played with Charlie Musselwhite. He a good friend of mine, a good harmonica player. He been here in Indianapolis, play at the Slippery Noodle, and send for me to come down there. Another boy, Mike Bloomfield, he play with Paul Butterfield. He worked for Bob Koester, sold records for him. And that's where a lot of 'em learned the blues from the black folks. Yeah, they sold them records. Mike Bloomfield was a good guitar picker, but he got to California and got on that stuff. Killed him.

All of 'em sell records for Bob Koester. That where they learned the blues, sellin' black folks' music. He had 'em hired, and they would learn how to play that stuff. So they went to playin' the blues and they got good at it.

I go to a lot of those schools to play, for the kids. They enjoyed it, some of 'em did. Went to play the Newport Festival in 1964. I had a record of that. A fella brought me a Newport Festival record. I and Sleepy John and Hammie played there. Hammie played the jug awhile and then he play the harp awhile. That was the biggest festival I ever been to, Newport Festival.

---

[1] *Chicago Style* was recorded in Chicago, August 16, 1979 (Delmark Records LP 649).

Taj Mahal

I went to California, me and Sleepy John. The guy met us on the bus, Los Angeles. His name was Taj Mahal. He said, "Y'all come on and stay with me. I know where the place at where y'all gonna play at." Say, "Y'all stay with me. I got a car. I'll carry ya where you got to go every night, and you'll save the hotel bill. Won't be as much." Well, he was a colored boy. We'll stay out and pay him, instead of goin' to a hotel, which we did. We stayed with him, so we were carried to this place. We didn't know nothin' about California, but he would carry us and bring us back.

So I was singing a song about "My baby left town, left me a mule to ride." When I left there he thought I said, "My baby caught the Katie, left me a mule to ride." He didn't get it good and straight. He made it, but he couldn't sell it until he put my name on it, Yank Rachell and Taj Mahal. Well, they paid him royalty. Well, I was gettin' royalty too. I got about ten thousand dollars out of it. The first check I got was ten thousand dollar, and I got that for three months. And then I started gettin' five thousand dollar every three months, three thousand dollar. So I decided to buy me another house. Well, I went and looked at a house. Woman said twenty-five hundred dollar down. Well, I paid that down on the house. The check come at the right time. I'm thinkin' about leavin' it though.

When he went to make the record, he couldn't do nothin' with it unless he put Yank Rachell name on it, so I get royalty like he does. And every now and then I get a check, but it been out so long, it don't be that much. But they still, the Blues Brothers, got that thing in their movie. Taj Mahal sing my song in their movie. Well, that's why I got my money out of it.

That's the only record company I got some money out of. Yeah, Taj Mahal play "She Caught the Katie." That's the only tune I know he did. His music, what I heard, is pretty good. He play some different kind of music, but I liked it. He come here once and we played together downtown there, some big place downtown. I forget the name of it, some big ballroom. And he play pretty good piano too, Taj Mahal does. I just play the mandolin.

I don't care what they play. I play it too. Any kind of piece they play, I play it. That's all it's to that. He play the blues. I play the blues, my blues, my way. Now they got a new style of blues they playin'. I don't fool with that. I play the old blues like I come up with, hard time blues, man, when you're choppin' cotton and pullin' corn, takin' a bath in them old tub like that.

Muddy Waters

I used to know Muddy. Yeah, Muddy bought two of my record, "Thirty-Eight Pistol Blues." He said he like 'em so well. I knowed Muddy Waters, Otis Spann, Otis Rush. Man, I know all of 'em. I never did play nothin' with him — just at a house sometimes. We meet at a blues festival. We go out and play something with one another. I never had a gig with him.

B. B. King

I never did do much playin' with him, but B. B. always give me respect. He honor me 'cause, see, I was in this business 'fore B. B. was, 'fore his time. But like I said, see, I didn't stop work to play music. See a lot of 'em, like B. B., put all his time in playin' music, you see, but I worked. I didn't put my time in playin' music. I always had a job, but I play music on my part-time. But B. B., if I had went out playin' like he was, I been just as famous, or more famous, than he was. But I wouldn't do that. I wouldn't go out playin' 'cause I had to take care of my kids and wife. But a lot of 'em wouldn't do nothin' but play music. You put all your time in music, well, that make it better for ya. Well, I didn't put my time all in music. I play music at night, daytime I work. That the way I do it all the time. I work up until, now I got sixty-five, I had to come out. Well, I ain't able to work right now 'cause I couldn't get a job, right now at eighty-six. That's the reason I can't drive now. I don't drive no more. I got a van at home and an Oldsmobile, but I can't drive.

Chapter 20

I went over there with Junior Wells, Little Brother Montgomery, Sippie Wallace, and, I don't know, a bunch of them. And we went over there. Then I come back; I went with Horst Lippman. And the next time I went, I went with Sunnyland Slim. I went 'bout four times.

I went to London, England, Paris, France, Czechoslovakia, Austria, Geneva, Baden-Baden. Two set of German over there. Yeah. And I went to Copenhagen, Switzerland, Holland, Amsterdam, you name it, and a lot of places I can't think of the name.

Russia, that's the worst place I ever been.[1] We went on a bus goin' through Russia. Them soldiers stopped that bus, kept us there four hours, before they let us move. Took a long cane, run it down the gas tank. Got on there and made everyone open their instrument, everybody had music, roll it down. Searched that bus all over, Russia did, 'fore we could go through. When we come back, we flew over Russia. Wouldn't come back on no bus. Yeah, that's a dandy. Was a bunch of men on that side and a bunch of men on t'other side. Had guns. Soldiers were walkin'. Damn! I was glad to get out of that place. Yeah, that's the worst place I ever been to.

We went to one place. Boys spent the night in a hotel. A pretty ashtray there, and the fool got it. They got ready to leave; some men come down figurin' to burn the bus down over that ashtray. I don't remember what country it was, but that boy got that ashtray and they were going to blow the bus up. Had to put that ashtray back. I said, "You bastard, you goin' get all of us killed." I was a scared man. I can't remember which country.

I know I been to the North Pole. That North Pole, be night there one week, daytime the next week. I went to Sweden, too, and Norway. Snow was so high there they had a bulldozer movin' it from the folks' door so they could get out. One thing, you better not spit. It's ice when it hit the ground! I had on two overcoats and them wadn't enough for me.

---

[1] Rachell is most likely referring to crossing the East German border, which was patrolled by Russian troops, to go to Berlin, where the American Folk Blues Festival had some performances.

The people there, they likes the music. They liked it. But, God knows, it's so cold. Man, I'm tellin' you true. I made a song about it: "So cold up north the bird can't hardly fly." Yessir, I recorded it. "So cold up north the bird can't hardly fly. I'm scared to go out door 'cause the wind cut the water out of my eye. I could stay in the north, but I ain't got sufficient clothes." Some of the boys say, "Oh, yes, ya know they sellin' clothes up here." That was the song, and then he answer me back, "I know." "I'm goin' back south until the winter gone. When winter gone then maybe I'll go back home." I done made this song up over there.[2]

They all right over there in Europe. We got big crowds. I went out and played places where B. B. had been. You go out and play, there be a big crowd there, but when you play your last piece, pow! Everybody gone. They don't hang around. No. They gone when you get through. You get up and go.

I play in clubs in Europe. Had a good audience in the clubs there. They enjoyed it. Course, lot of them didn't understand what we were playing there, but they tried to, though. You know they liked it, and so that the way that was. Had a good time there. Everybody treat you nice. They don't bother you, or nothin'. Yeah, they just look at you and smile.

Their language, I couldn't understand nothin'. One guy would go with us; he could talk American talk. But one day I got smart. I went somewhere; I wadn't gonna carry him with me. I was going by myself. Went into a cafe. The lady didn't know what I was sayin', I didn't know what she was sayin', and I just point at the stuff. She give it to me. I didn't know how much money it was. I put my hand in my pocket and give her a handful of money. She looked at it. She gave me some of it back. Well, I didn't know how much it was. I put it in my pocket. I set down and eat. Somethin' there in a jar, pretty stuff, look like somethin' good to eat. I put it on a sandwich. Man, it was so hot! Like to kill me right there.

We was on a bus goin' to play. I was with Tom Boyd; he was from California. He got me to carry some boys over there with me. Police got on the

---

[2] The song lyrics he quotes are from "Up North Blues." While they are certainly applicable to the weather he found in Scandinavia, Rachell recorded it for Blue Bird records in Chicago in 1941 with Sonny Boy Williamson. The song they recorded was based on the Sleepy John Estes recording of "Down South Blues" in 1935.

bus and one boy play the drum. He got on the bus and made us all get off the bus. Made us go to a little old house there, tumbledown little old place. Made us go there. Just one boy now, he made him pull off all his clothes. Didn't bother nobody but him. Made him pull all his clothes off. Didn't do nothin' to him. I don't know why he got at that boy like that. Pull us all off the bus, so we got late.

We went on the place. Settin' on a train, got to a place big as this house. Door come up like your garage door out there. *Whirrrr!* A big ship settin' out there. Well, this train run on that ship. That ship had railroad tracks on it. I thought it was gonna sink, all that train on there, trucks, iron everything. We got on that big ship. We were way out there on the water. Man, it had upstairs and downstairs. Upstairs they were gamblin'. One place they were cookin'; other place they were dancin'. It's somethin' to see. I been through somethin'. Wouldn't do it again for nothin'. I'm lucky to be livin'.

A man wanted me to go last year, and I wouldn't go. He offered me five thousand dollars, though. But I wouldn't go. I don't want to go to Europe no more. It's too much. You got to go through many thing before you go over there. You got to go here. You got to go there. Do this. Do that. They got to stamp that thing everywhere. Oh, man! They gonna know everything about you before you get over there! There's two set of German over there. To go from one to the other one, they got to look at this and stamp that. They got one set of German over here and the other set of German over there, and one set don't mix with the other. That's funny, but that's right.

Well, 'nother time a bunch of us went over there to Europe. Junior Wells and Otis Rush, we all went; Sleepy John and I went then. Hammie didn't go overseas with us, but I and John went. Went one place, we played, and the man had us back seven time. The other band was settin' there; they got mad. We'd play and we'd leave out. They go to pattin' and whistlin', go wild. I was playin' mandolin. John was playin' guitar. Man have us come back play 'nother song. Well, we was layin' somethin' on 'em.

There's a man wrote me from over there. Said, "Yank, I can get you all your royalty. I know about all your royalty." He said, "You got plenty royalty up there. You sign this paper and send it back to me." Well, I asked my lawyer about it, this colored girl named Judy. She wrote him a letter and he ain't wrote me no more. I got the paper at home right now. So, I didn't hear from him no more.

Well, I think the man wanted, you know, to use me or something. He send me a copy of me and John record, sent me two records that we made over there. He said, "I can get you your money." Said, "Blue Goose, Bluebird, Blind Pig, and Delmark." Well, you know, people'll use you if they can. Now them days is done. But since I got old I don't fool with that stuff much. I know now how people do ya. Lot of 'em will get something from you and make a thousand, a million dollar offen you, and you ain't got nothin', 'cept that hole in the pot.

Chapter 21

I hear a lot of people. A lot of people, they try to play my stuff, but they don't play it right. But I let 'em go ahead. They doin' the best they can. They gettin' by on it. I go to the Slippery Noodle down there. I go in there, man say, "Well, ladies and gentlemen, we got a legend in the house here, Yank Rachell." And some of 'em try and play my piece, mess it up. I don't say nothin', lessen they ask me. Let 'em go ahead with it. I ain't goin' to try and tell 'em nothin'. They get mad with me. But I know what's right with my piece, and I know what's wrong. If I made it, I know how I want it.

Well, after Shirley Griffith and J. T. Adams pass, I commenced to playin' around here with some younger people. I met Beki Brindle first, 'fore I knowed Larry DeMyer. Beki a little old girl. She about eighteen, I reckon, when I first met her. Leroy Bates, we were playin' together back then. So we run up on Beki. She had a guitar playin', so we got to playin'. She playin' pretty good, and I got to playin' with her. So I was called to go overseas, so Beki wanted to go. I said, "Your parents wouldn't want you to go overseas with me." So I asked her daddy.

He said, "Yes, she can go."

Then I met Larry. Larry knowed about me 'fore I knowed him. But I was gonna carry Beki overseas, but she was too young. Then she went to New York. So after she got back from New York, and her and Larry got married, I go over and play with them sometime.

Yeah, I tell you the truth. I played with so many guys, I met so many guys. Look like all of 'em try to hunt me, for some cause. I don't understand it. But since I been here I played with many a peoples here, white boys and colored boys. And lots of 'em play sample of my pieces now, you know. I teach 'em some how to play and do that. But I didn't mind it. Look like everybody like to play with me, so I try to help 'em the best I can. I appreciate it, you know. And I try to help 'em some 'cause I know I won't be here always.

I trained a lot of 'em, Beki, Pat Webb, Larry, Gordon Bonham, Stormy Johnson, Red Beans and Rice, Dave Morgan. We made a record together, call it "Pig Trader Blues." Well, all them different ones, I set down with 'em and try to teach 'em what I know, some of 'em. And they want me to go with 'em to play places. Sometime I don't feel like goin'. They enjoy me goin' with 'em. They want me to go to New York with 'em. But I'm not able to go. I have to have that dialysis. I wouldn't try and take that ride. Yeah, I done my part, I think.

Well Beki, she learn a lot from me. She went to New York and started playin' 'round up there. And she met John Sebastian, and she was talkin' about me, and he said, "Do you know him?"

And she said, "Yeah, I know him. He trained me a lot to play."

He said "He did?"

And she say, "He live in Indianapolis."

He say, "Well, I want to get in touch with him."

And that's the way he know me. So he came down here and played with me. Brought his band, I mean, all his guys. They record some with me, two songs, and we got to know John Sebastian. And we went to Memphis and played there at the W. C. Handy Awards. Yeah. Then he bought me a mandolin, paid sixteen hundred dollars for it, and gave it to me. I appreciated it. I needed it.

John Sebastian like to play with me. He come down here a lot of times. That's the third time he been here. He came here in April and we went to Memphis last time. Carry us down there to my hometown, Brownsville. Got me a room in the Peabody Hotel. So John Sebastian paid for all of that. Nice fella. He play harmonica, banjo, and guitar.

My Style of Music

Well, I ain't changed much. I like to play that old back down-home old stuff, you know. I play it, but I make it more modern. But it's on the same order of that. But I don't play the same piece all the time. I can get up there now and play something and you wouldn't know if I played it before. It come to me when I play. Rhyme up in my mind, way it used to do. But I don't do it like I used to.

I play what I sing. A lot of other players stroke it, but this is the way I learned. You play what you are singing. You watch B. B. King on TV. He sings and picks in the middle, but he don't play what he sings. That's my style. I play what I sing. But I got stiff and have to play it down now. When I was in better shape I played it up, all the time. Yeah, I liked that upstroke 'cause that the way I learned, quiverin'. I could do it that way, but goin' down I can't do that. I have to stroke it now to make notes.

Upstroke is the way I learned it though. That's the way you're supposed to go with a mandolin. After I got my hands stiff I have to play it down. I can't play that quiver like I used to. You can play that quiver better with an upstroke. Upstroke is a better sound to me. Sure is.

I play in C and G. That's the main ones on that mandolin. Playin' that other stuff is hard to play on a mandolin. But C and G, you play that better on a mandolin. But that B flat, or F sharp, I never could play that. I play the old blues on the mandolin. That what I play on the guitar, the old blues.

Acoustic guitar was the first thing I learnt. But when electric come in, that was something new to me, so I played that. I plugged my mandolin up into it. It sound good, so I went to playing electric all the time, you know. You don't play it hard. Electric is all right if you play it right. But you can play electric so it will blast you out. It won't sound right. Well, I know how to play electric and everything. On a mandolin you need electric, 'cause the strings is short.

Now that *Chicago Style* record, I was playing electric. But this last record me and Pat Webb and them made is acoustic. Well, it hard to play acoustic on a mandolin, make it sound right, because it's short and it ain't got no tone too much to it. But it play better when you play electric. But I play acoustic too. I play both of 'em. But I can play better with electric mandolin than I can acoustic. So guitar the same; you can turn it up and play it in a way it won't be blasting you. So that's the way that go. A lot of people play guitar and turn it up loud as they can get it. That don't sound right. I don't do that. I play my own style, nobody's style but mine.

The record I just made with Pat Webb and Allen Stratyner is all acoustic. I don't like to play 'coustic anymore. It didn't have enough bass in it for me, but I played like they wanted. Playing acoustic on the mandolin you can't get what you get if you're playin' electric. But it didn't have no bass. Guitar, harmonica, and mandolin. The harmonica and mandolin played all right, but you ought to have some heavy stuff in there. But I did what they wanted to do. They wanted the old-time sound, so it's all right. It's a pretty nice tape. Call it *Too Hot for the Devil*.[1] Got my song: "Hello world, anybody see my Ida B? She too hot for the devil, but God know she just right for me."

But I like that *Chicago Style* better than I do any of 'em. *Chicago Style* is electric, and I could play the mandolin better with electric. You ain't got to blast and play loud with electric; you can play like you always, like acoustic. Some of 'em don't understand and they play too loud. They play rock and roll and think they're playin' blues, but they ain't. There's a difference between the blues and rock and roll. That what I think. I play both of 'em. But a lot of people go, "I'm a blues player," but they playin' rock and roll. Blues is somethin' quiet and mellow, sad. That's what the blues is.

A guy playin' rock and roll, he think he playin' the blues. Buhhh! Them ain't no blues. That rock and roll. Blues is slow and easy, you know, slow. They got to get out them electric guitars and things and turn it up loud. *Wah! Wah! Wah!* That ain't no blues. I don't say nothin' to 'em, you know. I

---

[1] Recorded in Indianapolis, Indiana, in 1997 (Flatrock Records FRCD-16).

let 'em go right ahead. The announcer says, "Ladies and gentlemen, such an such a blues player!" And they turn it up real loud then. But that ain't no blues playin', to me.

Everybody don't know how to play the blues. To my eye they don't. I don't play nothin' like nobody. I play my own way, my own thoughts and everything, 'cause you can't please everybody. People got different ideas about things. Everybody don't like the same thing. Some people'll say, "Oh, he can play." Some other people say, "I don't like his playing." See, that's the way the world go. Yeah. Some people don't like my playin' maybe. But it don't make me no difference. Somebody like it, some don't, so I'm gonna do the best I can.

B. B. King play the blues. You catch a lot 'em tryin' to imitate him playin' the blues, but they don't have the feeling B. B. has. B. B. feel the blues. Lot of them play his pieces but they don't feel it. I like him 'cause he play his own style, and I play my style. I don't play like B. B. I went to playin' one night, settin' down playin', and a lady come out there say, "Hi, you sure sound good! Can you play B. B. King?"

I said, "Yeah, if you put some strings on him, I'll play him."

I'm Yank Rachell. I ain't no B. B. King! But B. B. always honor me, and he like to hear me play. And he's called me every now and then.

Chapter 22

Last January they had a concert here in Indianapolis. All my music friends did it for me to raise some money to help me out and show 'preciation for how I trained 'em all. It was really nice, best I ever had, and I really enjoyed it. Help me some. I been in bad shape. I been way behind.

But I had a nice time all right. There were over two hundred people there. Everybody was so nice. No one had a cross word. Just set down and enjoy the music. John Sebastian was down with his band. I played some with them. Then Larry and my granddaughter, we played some. Yeah. Maenell, my baby daughter, and Willa B. and my granddaughters Sheena and Tracy, they sang and folks enjoyed it. They got a gospel group. They sung one song up there and everybody went to pieces on it.

I played old blues; it's what I used to playin'. That's what they like, that old down-home stuff. A lot of stuff I play ain't been played. I rhyme it up. I got all kind of stuff I can play, way-back stuff, later stuff, yeah, "Divin' Duck," "Tappin' That Thing," ".38 Pistol Blues," "Army Man Blues," "Goin' to Brownsville, Take the Right-Hand Road," all that old stuff, 'cause people like that now. Lot of 'em hadn't heard it. They didn't understand it. I don't go play what other people play. I play what I play. I play my own style.

The money helped some 'cause I ain't got no way to go nowhere, no transportation. My granddaughter Sheena, she do my driving, but she live in Castleton. She can't come in to Indianapolis all the time and I can't go there. So, it's hard for me to get around. I had a van. It's in the shop three months, but he ain't done nothin'. I paid some money, but it's still there. I have to have friends take me to dialysis. Larry DeMyer takes me a lot. Another guy, you got to pay him four or five dollars to carry you and bring you back. I ain't able to work nowhere. My breath's too short. I'm too old to work anyhow. I'm eighty-six years old.

My income is $600 a month. I have to pay $525 a month rent and then the light bill, telephone bill, heat. That keep me strained up good. Maenell get a little check from her husband's pension, but you get it and it's gone.

WHY SOMEONE SINGS THE BLUES

Well, feeling sad will make you sing the blues. You're downhearted and everybody against ya, and don't want to pay you no attention. Everything go wrong; nothin' go right. That'll give ya the blues. That what it is. Some people say I'm bored. You ain't bored; ya got the blues. Little baby have the blues in the cradle. He cryin', cryin', cryin', you don't give 'em something. You give 'em what he want, he be all right. You sing the blues; it help ya. Helped me.

A lot of white people, they ain't had no hard times, don't have the blues. Black folk had a hard time. They ain't done nothin' but sing the blues, see? But that where the blues came from, hard times and don't have nothin'. Nothin' go your way, you have to have the blues. Hell, I had the blues so long they've turned into the blacks.

Well, younger peoples, tell you the truth, they're not playin' no blues. They sing the blues and playin' rock and roll. The younger people don't know nothin' about no blues. But the blues is from your heart. That's why the blues is from your soul. But these people hear the blues, they playin' it, but they don't feel it. Lot of 'em go play the blues, they don't feel the blues. When I get up there and play the blues, I feel the blues. I feel like cryin'. Them the blues. Yeah, I'm tellin' ya now what I know. They go around with a guitar, say, "I'm a blues player." He ain't no blues player. He'll play it, but he don't feel it. He just playin' what he heard somebody play what had the blues. But he don't have no blues. I feel it when I got the blues. I really feel it. I don't have the blues like I used to, but I can play the blues sometime now.

BLUES ALWAYS WILL BE

There will always be the blues. It will never go out, the old, original blues. Blues always will be. I and Sleepy John the first one come out playing the old, real down-home blues. That been many years ago. And so people pick it up and go ahead and play it their way. Put something to it their way. But the real old, down-home blues, that's all there is. Ain't nothin' gonna beat it. I don't care what you do. I don't care about rock and roll and all that stuff. The blues the end of it. The blues is something. Yeah.

I like jazz, good jazz. Wes Montgomery a good guitar player. I wadn't too much 'quainted with him. I knew about him and he knew about me. Met him a few times. But then he passed.

You play jazz, I like to hear good jazz. But I'd rather hear the blues. That rock and roll went from rock and roll to this rap. You know this rap, I don't fool with it. I turn it off. I don't want to hear no rap. The younger dudes come up with that stuff, they don't know nothin'. But the older people like the blues. Rap. That's in, but the blues is always going to stand, like jazz. Jazz will stand and the blues will never go out, 'cause so many people know the blues. So many people have the blues. Some of 'em have it but they can't play it, but they have it.

Oh, I don't know. I just born way back in the country. Didn't have nothin'. That's where the blues come from. One pair of shoe a year. Sole wear out, put paper on the bottom of your shoe. Keep your foot off the ground. One pair of pants, blue jean, fifty cent. Shirt a quarter. I come on, they didn't have no light, didn't have no light through the world, nowhere. Be dark. I'm tellin' ya, I wouldn't take nothin' for what I done learned, but I done forgot so much. I been through a heap in my day. Sure have. So anything you can think of, I'll tell ya best that I know. I'll tell ya the truth about it. I got old now. I can't do nothin' like I used to.

White Folks

The white people gettin' to the blues now. Lot of white people like the blues. They just learnin' what the blues were. See, they didn't know nothin' about no blues. Didn't have no hard times. Didn't have nothin' to worry about. But colored people had a hard time. Way back, they didn't have nothin', and they didn't have nothin' but the blues. But white people born, have plenty money. Didn't have to worry 'bout no blues or nothin'. They didn't suffer for nothin', you know, like the black people did. But now they like the blues; they learn the blues.

I have ta tell ya, now I got so old, white people been mighty nice to me. I have to give it to them. If it wadn't for them, I wouldn't have made it to now. Larry, and Pat Webb, and different ones, all of 'em help me. The cost of livin' so high it got me on the grindin' stone.

Old and in the Way

The blues is—one time I had a cryin' spell, I don't know how come it was, and I went in there cryin'. My daughter ask, "What's the matter?" I just felt downhearted. Felt I was throwed away. Felt like nobody didn't want me.

I'm old and people have to do for me. Always did for myself. Never had to go to nobody for nothin' much. Always had transportation and plenty clothes, and everything, but now I can't get that stuff. But that hurt me. I had the blues; I had to cry. I think about it now, I don't know what to think.

Well, it look like I'm in the way. Somebody have to help me, you know. I'm not used to that. I'm used to doin' for my own self, and it look like I'm botherin' people. But they say, "No Yank, you ain't botherin' us. We want to do that for you. You deserve that." But I feel like I ought could do it myself. But I can't. And I shouldn't worry about it.

This dialysis thing sure take up a lot of time. I got to be on it Tuesday, Thursday, and Saturday. If I hadn't a been on it I wouldn't a been livin' now, 'cause I was swelled up. My kidney ain't workin'. Can't make no water. That thing draw the water out you, carry you back and forth. You don't feel nothin'; you just set there. But if it draw too much water out, your hand get stiff. You can't move it. Your voice leave you. You can't do nothin'. You cramp. So, I woke up one mornin', I was swell up everywhere. My private was swelled up like a bladder. I couldn't put my leg together. All my leg was swell up. Now I done lost so much weight all my shoe too big. I got four, five pair good shoe. They too big, but I can't throw 'em away. I just wear 'em anyway. Let 'em flop. I don't care. But I'm still livin'. Yeah.

I'm well blessed to be here. I get to thinkin' about that. The Lord blessed me to be here. But I always try to do the right thing with my family, and treat everybody right. I got a lot of white friends. They helped me, carryin' me. I treat 'em right; they treat me right. I know we all here together. We got to live here together. I don't hate nobody. There was a fella across the street, he just moved, he didn't like black folks. He wouldn't speak, he wouldn't do anything. The other neighbor next door, he's friendly.

That guy moved, I'm glad he left. He didn't want you to play your music. Somebody was goin' to hurt him if he hadn't a left. So I didn't bother with him.

All Them Fellas Gone

I ain't never been in this shape before. But you never know what shape you goin' to get in before you leave this world. You know that? That's right.

You never know. I don't know I'd ever be in this shape, have to walk with a cane, arthritis and all of that. Well, I wadn't used to that. But after I got older to the age I am, I think I'm lucky to be living. I don't know. Eighty-six years old. Sixteen of March I'll be eighty-seven, if I live to see that. Well, there been so many of 'em been here and gone since I been here. So many of my musicianers, most of 'em is gone. Sleepy John Estes, Hammie Nixon, Tommy Gary, Walter Davis, Sonny Boy and Joe Williams, Shirley Griffith, J. T. Adams, all them fellas gone.

Appendix 1

Comments on Yank Rachell's Mandolin Style

Rich DelGrosso

Without the benefit of a teacher or mentor, Yank Rachell learned to play on his own. He did have knowledge of the standard tuning of the instrument (high to low, E-A-D-G: each successive pair of strings is tuned a fifth below the pair of strings before it). But he didn't tie himself to convention, and his tuning and his picking style developed to meet his own needs. I still remember when I sat down with a Rachell recording, one where he was playing with Sleepy John Estes. I picked up my mandolin and found that he was playing in the key of E. For mandolin players E is not an easy key in which to play! What further amazed me were the sounds he was getting in this key, sixth chords with open strings! Bass doublestops with open strings! In E!

After meeting Yank and watching him play, the mystery of the tuning was immediately solved. Rachell, who grew up tuning the instrument by ear, followed the convention of tuning by fifths, but he often tuned his instrument to his voice in his range for singing. Thus the fourth pair of strings, which classical mandolin players tune to G (below middle C), Rachell often tuned to E, or F or F#. This tuning would place the instrument, if tuned to E, one and a half steps below pitch, and the "G chord" would sound in E. The tuning accounts for the bass riffs one hears in "Shotgun Blues," where the riff is supported by a droning open fourth pair of strings. It also explains the chiming C# above the full chord, as Rachell often emphasized the E chord with an open first string (C#).

With this tuning, the key of E is played in the G position, and A is played in the C position. Both of these keys are commonly used in the blues, especially by guitar players. Rachell had learned the proper naming of notes and keys but did not take into account his lowered tuning. As a result, when he played in the G position, he called it G, even though his instrument sounded in the key of E! It made jamming with him really challenging. I remember distinctly a jam session where I played guitar and acted as a chord interpreter for the band. But what a great sound! I had never heard a mandolin hold its own against a guitar in the blues before. The lower pitch brought the mandolin down into the range of the guitar, and the two really blended well. The mandolin's doubled strings gave it a trill that the guitar lacked, but the two together on the bass really rocked!

I also noted that Rachell used a different picking style than was the convention. He picked primarily with upstrokes, even on triplet runs! The force gained by the upstroking made the strings ring out loud, but it also changed the order of sounded strings, making the first and second pairs dominant over the third and fourth. Another great sound!

The mandolin became popular in the South in the late nineteenth century, about the same time people began playing blues. In general, very few performers tried to carry the mandolin from its string band roots into the mainstream of blues performing and recording. However, the mandolin does appear on records at the beginning of the era of recorded blues in the 1920s. This is due to the fact that blues singers often brought musicians from their local string bands to accompany them on their recording sessions. As a result, mandolin accompaniment can be heard on blues recordings that Furry Lewis, Peg Leg Howell, Ishman Bracey, Sleepy John Estes, and others made between 1927 and 1930.

With the exception of Rachell, only one performer sustained a lengthy recording career performing blues on the mandolin in the pre–World War II period, Charlie McCoy. He began his career in the 1920s by playing mandolin and guitar in Mississippi string bands, sometimes with members of the multitalented Chatmon family. He recorded as a member of the Mississippi Hot Footers and the Mississippi Mud Steppers in 1929 and 1930. During the 1930s McCoy worked as a sideman on recordings by a variety of blues singers as well as with a jazz and blues band called the Harlem Hamfats. Like Rachell, he doubled on mandolin and guitar. McCoy's recording work ceased with the outbreak of World War II, making Rachell the only recorded blues mandolinist from the prewar era, with the exception of Willie Hatcher, to continue to perform and record with the instrument after World War II.[1]

---

[1] Carl Martin recorded pre- and postwar, but only with the mandolin postwar. Johnny Young presumably played prewar, but didn't record.

Appendix 2

Comments on Yank Rachell's Guitar Style

David Evans

The key to understanding Yank Rachell's guitar style is accepting and appreciating the fact that most of his playing was done in the company of other musicians. It would be wrong to try to force him into the stereotyped role of a solo country bluesman who just happened to perform a lot with others. Instead, he was essentially a band musician who had a vestigial solo guitar style that was scarcely documented in his recordings. In his first recording session in 1929, barely nineteen years old, he is a member of the Three Js band, and in 1934 he came to New York to record as a member of the Jackson Shieks, a string trio. For some reason the violinist of the latter group didn't play on any of the six pieces that were issued from this session, with the result that we hear Rachell as a solo guitarist on one track and in a guitar duet on the others. He would not record again in these formats until the 1960s and 1970s, and most of that playing is a result of the conscious effort of the producers of one of his albums to get him to recall his solo repertoire.

For the bulk of his musical career Rachell displayed a single guitar style that appears limited in some respects but actually proves to be quite versatile, enabling him to perform with an idiosyncratic blues pianist like Walter Davis and a star of blues harmonica like Sonny Boy Williamson. Almost all of his playing was set in the G position of standard tuning. This is not a particularly common key for solo country blues guitarists, but it was favored by string band guitarists in the South, both black and white, and it remains in common use in bluegrass bands. It is from his string band background that Rachell no doubt acquired his fondness for the G position on the guitar. To play in higher keys he simply used a capo, playing as high as the key of C (capo on the fifth fret). There were few exceptions to this practice. His first issued recording with guitar from 1934, "Blue and Worried Woman," is possibly in open A tuning (high to low, E-C#-A-E-A-E), although his playing is in many ways like his work in G of standard tuning. On "Stack o' Dollars," also from 1934, he plays in the C position of standard tuning, another key favored by string band musicians and one that would be developed by fellow Brownsville guitarists Sleepy John Estes and Charlie Pickett. Rachell also plays in C position on Sonny Boy Williamson's "I'm Tired Trucking My Blues Away" from 1938. Not until 1973 would Rachell again depart from the G position in his recordings. In that year his producers extracted from him two performances in E position and one in D. One of those in E, "Pack My Clothes and Go," seems actually to be an attempt to sound modernistic on the guitar in a display of string bending. The other piece, however, "Matchbox Blues," is quite archaic and is evidently a version of the earliest guitar blues he could remember. It represents essentially a style that Rachell rejected, and he recalls it with some difficulty on his recording. "Wadie Green" is played in the D position and also has an archaic flavor. Rachell normally performed it with mandolin, having converted it to that instrument by 1930, although his recording of it from that year remains unissued.

Within the G position of standard tuning Rachell's playing was quite versatile. Whether he was doing the singing or accompanying someone else, his guitar playing, like his mandolin work, often paraphrased the vocal line heterophonically (see chapter 4), filling in the breaks with improvised responses. He didn't use the common device among country blues guitarists of an alternating bass pattern, nor were his notes obviously suggested by left-hand chord positions, and most of his tunes did not contain a "signature" riff. In many respects his playing was in the same spirit as that of a modern lead guitarist who improvises series of notes without holding a chord position and varies his instrumental passages throughout the performance.

This improvisational approach was strongly allied to a remarkable rhythmic flexibility, which is perhaps the most outstanding characteristic of Rachell's playing. Within a single performance he would play passages of a chopped chord in quarter notes, switching at times to "swing" eighth notes (pairs of eighth notes in which the first note is somewhat more emphatic and longer that the second). This rhythmic approach is very likely derived from a left-hand piano technique that came into vogue in the late 1920s and early 1930s among barrelhouse pianists such as Roosevelt Sykes. Among guitarists who recorded in this period, the technique is also heard in the work of Henry Townsend and Peetie Wheatstraw, both from St. Louis (as was Sykes); and both of them are also pianists who used the same approach on that instrument. Rachell went to St. Louis in the 1930s and knew all of these musicians, although it is not known whether he had already interacted with them by the time of his 1934 recording session when he first displayed this guitar technique. To this basic rhythm of quarter notes and swing eighths, Rachell would add passages of eighth-note triplets or of sixteenth notes, in the latter case sometimes causing the entire ensemble to move into double time. By the time of his 1938 recording session he had added mandolin-like tremolos to his guitar technique. At this point it becomes very difficult for the listener to distinguish between his guitar and mandolin playing on recordings. Other guitarists who used tremolo technique were Blind Lemon Jefferson, Charlie McCoy, and Carl Martin, of whom the latter two (and possibly Jefferson as well) were also mandolinists. Some outstanding examples of Rachell's rhythmic flexibility on the guitar are heard in his 1938 accompaniment to Sonny Boy Williamson's "Deep Down in the Ground" (itself a version of Rachell's 1934 "Stack o' Dollars") and his own "Rainy Day Blues" of 1941, where he inspires the whole ensemble to vary the rhythm.

The characteristics described above might be said to represent a middle period in the evolution of Yank Rachell's guitar style, lasting from around

1934 to 1941 or perhaps later. An earlier period of more archaic and more conventional country blues solo guitar style can be detected in his 1973 recordings of "Matchbox Blues" and "Wadie Green," which were attempts to extract the oldest layer of his repertoire, and in odd items from his middle period, such as the riff-based "Peach Tree Blues" from 1941. Sometime between 1941 and his first "rediscovery" sessions of 1963–65, his guitar playing came under the influence of the new electric guitar style that had been pioneered in the 1940s by T-Bone Walker and other artists. This style, influenced by jazz guitar, alternated rhythmic playing featuring seventh and ninth chords with darting improvisational lead lines full of string bending. While Rachell's middle period style had already anticipated some of these developments, he added some of the new chords and string bending to his other techniques in the key of G. This late period style can be heard on his accompaniment to Sleepy John Estes' 1965 "Government Money" and his own 1973 acoustic guitar performance of "Des Moines, Iowa." During this revival phase of his career, however, Rachell was mostly encouraged to play the mandolin. His new guitar style tended to be viewed by others as second-rate lead playing rather than an interesting combination of influences from country blues guitar, barrelhouse piano, mandolin, and jazzy electric lead work. His only guitar-oriented recording session during this period was an (albeit worthwhile) exercise in archaism, while a 1979 attempt to record him in an electric "Chicago" blues style found him playing only mandolin in an ensemble that featured another electric guitarist. There are thus no issued recordings of Yank Rachell playing electric guitar in a post–World War II electric ensemble, recordings by which we might judge the effectiveness of his adaptation to this format. One can only hope that such recordings exist on tape and will surface someday. Meanwhile, we have much to enjoy and admire in the rest of his recorded guitar playing.

Appendix 3

Interviews

The following are interviews conducted with musicians and colleagues who knew, worked with, or were influenced by Yank Rachell.

HENRY TOWNSEND

Born in Shelby, Mississippi, in 1909, Henry Townsend has had a long career as a blues pianist, guitar player, and vocalist. He lives in St. Louis and is still performing. His autobiography, A Life in the Blues *(University of Illinois Press) was published in 1999.*

When I first met Yank it was in the latter part of the 1930s in St. Louis. Yank was living here. He was employed, and later he left. I know Yank worked for some kind of a steel company. At that time I was Walter Davis' backup man, and Yank had done some work with Walter Davis too, and he was kind of undecided as to which one of us he really wanted to work with. We both could work with him as successful on certain things. And that's when I first met Yank.

Well, there were a few clubs where I and Yank played together in St. Louis in 1939 and 1940. I'm callin' them clubs now, but they were more or less speakeasies and so forth. Yank played a lot of guitar back then; he wasn't heavy on mandolin at all.

Big Joe Williams at that time was in and out of St. Louis. All three of us played together from time to time, not all together at once, but he'd play with me and then with Yank in public places. He was hard to get along with. We never really did fall out or anything, 'cause I knew his mentality and never tried to bother his nerves at all. Big Joe was suspicious because there was so much he wanted to know but didn't know and was afraid of. He'd try to make sure that nobody was doin' him, and he didn't have much confidence in his own self and that would make him a little bit of a cantankerous guy. He would go ahead and fulfill the obligation if you treat him the way he wanted to be treated. And a lot of times it would be unneeded, but that was Big Joe. He and I never had any problems.

John Lee Williamson came through St. Louis quite often then. John Lee was one of the fellas that would come through and spend time with me. I was, I guess, pretty much a safe haven when he went to St. Louis. He'd just come on in and I'd be unaware of it, but he knew he had a place to settle himself. He'd come in and stay with me.

Yank's style of blues and mine was similar. He and I had a lot in common in the music field, that's why we worked so well together. That song that he made, "Divin' Duck," I believe was the title, that's one I like the best of Yank's. I liked the way Yank worked with me very much, very much.

I made a recording for the Nighthawk Record Company; *Mule* was the title. Yank played with me on several cuts on that album. It was recorded here in St. Louis. I don't think it's available too much.

I recorded with Yank in his home town in Indianapolis. I don't know; it could have been five, six years ago. I never heard anything about the recording. I don't know if it had ever been released or not. The last time I talked to him he couldn't give me any information on it.

Yank was a beautiful person. He was not cantankerous at all, and very considerate of other people, very easy to get along with. Oh, he had a lot of ambition. He was highly ambitious, but he was about as nice a person as you would want to meet. That is the way he and I got along.

We traveled quite a bit together. We done some days in California not too long ago. It was he and his granddaughter, and my wife. We toured California, and we were booked together as a team several other places. And he was a beautiful fella.

I think the tour was in the seventies; I don't remember exactly. That tour was for blues festivals. I'm reasonably sure it was a festival type of thing. His granddaughter was workin' with us at that time [Sheena Rachell played electric bass] and my wife was a vocalist.

ROBERT KOESTER

Robert Koester is the owner of Delmark Records and the Jazz Record Mart, both located in Chicago. For decades they have been important institutions for preserving and developing blues and jazz. Sleepy John Estes was believed by many to be dead until Koester recorded him in the early sixties. Through Estes he was able to contact Yank Rachell.

Well, as soon as we found John, I started running down the list of people he'd recorded with and he told me Yank was living in Indianapolis. So, first time we brought John up to record it just was solo; we just did sort of an exploratory session. And, as I recall, he had fifty-odd tunes at that time. We used maybe half a dozen of them. Then he came back with Hammie and we had a bass and piano and finished the first album [*The Legend of Sleepy John Estes*, 1962, Delmark 603].

I wanted to record Yank, but I had to move the record store around that time. It sort of complicated things. But eventually we did record Yank, and I remember that session, the *Mandolin Blues* session (recorded in 1963, Delmark DL-606), was kind of hectic because it was recorded at a guy's house on the west side. An amateur, well, he was a professional electrical engineer, but not a professional recording engineer.

We were going to meet at the store to go out to the session. And the night before, Big Joe Williams turned up. He used to sleep in the basement of the Jazz Record Mart, which was my main source of livelihood. He had a key to the place. Anyway, he had shown up in town and I ran into him the night before the record date on Wells Street—which was then the music street, the hippie street.

So there were quite a few places there with music, one of which was the Plugged Nickel, and Little Brother Montgomery had a band there. This was before they went into the big name thing and eventually Miles Davis made his records there. Little Brother had a six-piece Dixieland band there. Joe was in the habit of going over there to visit Brother. At this time he had that old Silvertone guitar and he got very drunk.

And I remember Mayo Williams, the guy who had been the producer for Paramount and Black Patti, Vocalion and Decca, etcetera, had been there. And he kind of congratulated me on being able to record Big Joe. He had made the mistake of having Big Joe play with Little Brother. Brother wouldn't bend; he was twelve bars, man. That meant twelve bars. That meant forty-eight beats! No country time!

Anyway, that night Joe took exception with what Mayo said and wanted to hit him over the head with his Silvertone. Joe was like that. He would get very drunk and get very belligerent. It wouldn't take much to set him off. I just walked away. And we had the session the next day and Joe wasn't particularly invited. It didn't occur to me to add him to the date. Then I figured he'd be hung over and he'd be no damn good anyway.

So Yank and John and Hammie were staying at someone's home on the south side, and the guy who they were staying with was going to bring them down to the store so we could then go out to this guy's house to record. I had my Crown tape recorder. Another guy brought in some good mikes and—no John, no Hammie, no Yank. They hadn't shown up. We couldn't figure out what to do, so I believe I left instructions at the store on the location of the house. It was West Monroe, if I remember correctly, way out pretty far on West Monroe, which at that time was a white neighborhood; it was black several years later. So I said, so it shouldn't be a total loss, "Joe, why don't you come along?" And Mike Bloomfield was there. We had had one session at Mike Bloomfield's house. But we couldn't have the second session there, because Yank's big foot stompin' on the floor had knocked some plaster off the ceiling downstairs. Pete Welding was there for the first session but not the second one.

Anyway, we went out to this guy's house. And so to do something to just fool around, 'cause we had arranged for everything, we decided to just do some things for Joe and Mike. And we set up and were ready to record, and here they come, the three stragglers! It seems there'd been some fight at this massive apartment on South Parkway, now Martin Luther King Drive, where John or Hammie or Yank would stay whenever they were in town. Real nice people, but they'd had a big row the night before. They possibly had a row with the musicians, 'cause as soon as Hammie or John would show up, the place would be like a barrelhouse, a house party night and day. And I imagine somebody wanted to get some sleep. I don't know what the trouble was, but they had either been kicked out or had decided to leave and stay somewhere else. And when they did that they lost their ride down to the session.

Anyway, they showed up and we did the date and that's why Joe and Mike are on it. And there's one Joe Williams vocal because we were starting to record that song by Joe and he said, "I'll do it with the band and you can put it on the album and pay me a little something for it." It was a pretty good session.

It was the first time I noticed that Hammie really didn't know how to blow a jug. He didn't understand the concept of blowing across the mouth. He would just make this sound with his lips and would blow the jug any old way. He'd play it upside down, sideways. He did a big show about twirling the jug as he played.

For the release of *Mandolin Blues*, I thought, "Jesus, we've had Dave Van Ronk with his jug band and we've had Kweskin's band and Victoria Spivey got a band together, the Even Dozen Jug Band." These jug bands probably never existed outside the studio. It was kind of a sell thing. I thought a real jug band record might do a little number for Yank. He could get into royalties. But I had a lot of bad experiences with the folkies, the folk music hierarchy. In fact, Mr. Von Rank was quoted, and this is from Pete Welding, he was telling them, the folk music magazines, "This is no good. You don't want to review this record." And it was listed, one line, "Yank Rachell, *Mandolin Blues*." It didn't say anything about it being a jug band record and it kind of was. I think it would have been deserving of some mention. *Mandolin Blues* probably sold six, seven, or eight hundred first year out.

I've always been a little bit surprised that, given all the mandolins that had been sold in those years, that there weren't more mandolin players. But there don't seem to be but a handful of guys that played the instrument. It makes him unique, just by force of history. I think he's one of the best, to me one of the most interesting. I can hear in my mind's ear Yank playing. And I've listened to an awful lot of Charlie McCoy records, and I don't really remember much. Of course, I didn't have the advantage of hearing him play live. But I did have the advantage of hearing a lot of Johnny Young. He was around Chicago, and I don't really remember him having that much of a unique style. A lot of quintupling. So I think Yank had a pretty good position.

I think, to me, John was a more important artist, because of his writing and because of his unique singing sound. Now Yank has kind of a unique voice, but he doesn't have — not that much soul as there is with John. Yank's a straighter guy. Yank's the kind of guy who worked in a defense plant in World War II. I hate to think what John did during World War II, probably drank. Yank looks like, you put that pipe in his mouth, and he looks like he owns the local hardware store, whereas John was just a scamp, man, just a runaround. But Yank was a substantial guy.

It was often the case that Yank had to keep the other musicians sober enough to finish a job. It used scare the hell out of me to see the way John would go at it when we'd be partying. But I have to tell you, the best I heard in my life was at those parties on South Parkway. He would howl! It was amazing. We never caught John that good. We caught him good, but we never caught him that good.

We still have tapes of John and of Yank that haven't been released. I'd like to go through them sometime and release some more of them. One thing is that the mandolin Yank used on a lot of those sessions was really shitty. I don't know that the quality would be good enough to release.

I went to the Newport festival with John, Hammie, and Yank in 1964. Man, I had to sleep in the same room with those guys and the farting and the snoring! I learned that Hammie grinds his teeth; they must have been gone before he was. Alan Lomax's people slept in the hotel; Muddy Waters slept in the hotel. There was this house that they rented, and everybody was given army cots to sleep on. Bukka White, Fred and Annie McDowell, and Son House were there too. Also there was Jesse Fuller, who preferred to sleep in his car with a shotgun over his shoulder. And then John, Hammie, Yank, and Skip James were there too. God, I forget who else. There were some others. I just thought they were not treated all that well. Although they did let us, massa did let us, go up to the big house for breakfast every morning. And Lomax conned Estes into joining his troupe on the stage one night for no extra money. Everybody got fifty bucks a day. I didn't get any money. I just went along for the free admission.

And the Vanguard deal wasn't too bad, for the record. But there was a certain lack of respect. My God, they had cornered most of the great blues talent in the city.

John and Hammie and Yank got a gig in a waterfront bar to pick up some spare money. I think it might have been two nights. I only went one night. But I was amazed it was a waterfront bar in Newport with a predominately, but not entirely, black crowd. But apparently it was a bar catering to black tastes, and they went over real well. It was a blues band, Hammie, Yank, and John. And I recall Yank played mostly guitar that night and it went over awfully well, with the kind of people who had forgotten about blues back in 1941.

CHARLIE MUSSELWHITE

Charlie Musselwhite was born in Kosciusko, Mississippi, in 1944. A blues harmonica player, he regularly records and plays club dates and music festivals. As a teenager he played at local clubs in Chicago with many established bluesmen, including Yank Rachell, Homesick James, Johnny Young, and Robert Nighthawk. He recorded his first album in 1968. Musselwhite begins by speaking about the time he first met Rachell.

Well, he was livin' in Indianapolis, but he was making regular trips to Chicago to play at the Fickle Pickle and some other places. He might have played at Mother Blues. He came mostly just to visit, not just to work. He'd come up when Hammie Nixon and Sleepy John were up there from Brownsville and visit with them, and hang out at the Jazz Record Mart in the back and hang out with Big Joe Williams. Me and Yank, we'd go around and we'd take cabs and take buses and go see whoever was playin', like Muddy Waters and Howlin' Wolf and Homesick James.

He just liked to go out and see people, hear the music. He enjoyed it, just really had a good time. He'd have a few drinks but never really got drunk that I recall. Always held his liquor, not like some of those guys. They would turn into real monsters. He had an even personality, didn't go through swings, you know. Didn't have a chip on his shoulder. Wasn't bitter. Well, he might have been pissed off about things, but he just was a nice guy. Always really dressed sharp, and enjoyed people, enjoyed a good laugh. Just a real pleasant man.

It was in the early sixties and I was working in a record store, or playing music on the side, or starving, you know, depending on what day it was. I worked at the Jazz Record Mart for a while; then I got in an altercation with Koester and left. And Big Joe was livin' there too. And there was another record store on Wells Street, in Old Town, on the corner of Stiller and Wells, or near the corner. And it was called the Old Wells Record Shop. And the guy that owned that place drove a cab in the daytime, so I would sit up there. Big Joe moved over there too, 'cause there were rooms in back of the record store. So me and Joe would sit around there all day, while this guy drove the cab, and I'd be off at night. Yank would come over there too, and we'd just sit around and play records, always a little drinkin' going on too, just socializing. And at night we'd go out and see people. Find out who was playin' where.

Sleepy John Estes had some relative; I don't know if he was a cousin or an uncle, but his name was Peter Peete. And he had like the world's greatest laugh, and we'd go over to Peter Peete's house, and Sleepy John and Hammie would be there and people would come by to visit. I remember Willie Dixon and different musicians would come by there. It was a lot of socializing and hangin' out and an occasional gig at these little folk places, like the Fickle Pickle.

I went to Chicago when I was eighteen. That was in '62. So I was a teenager, early twenties. And they accepted me and we just went off and had a great time. Often it was just me and Yank. He was pretty adventurous. I'd say, "So and so is playin' over at the so and so club. You want to go?" He'd say, "Yeah. Let's go."

It was like sort of an unspoken thing that Yank would restore order if things got too rowdy. I thought that everybody understood that he was the guy that really was the smartest one of the group. And he was well respected. People always listened if he started talking. If the situation was getting out of hand, or he had something to say, they would stop and listen to him. And they would concede that he had the best idea about whatever was happening. At the same time, he never acted liked he was superior, or a boss, or threw his weight around. You know what I mean? He was looked up to. And he was respected as a musician, too.

Well, he played guitar quite a bit besides mandolin. I just figured mandolin was one of the instruments he learned. Maybe there were more mandolin players when he was young. There were only three that I knew of, and I knew all three of them, and that was Willie Hatcher, Johnny Young, and Yank Rachell. Maybe I'm forgetting somebody.

I always enjoyed his playing and I really enjoyed his singing too, and the tunes he did. I always wondered if the "Skinny Mama" that Sonny Boy recorded is the same one Yank sang, because he started recording years before Sonny Boy. So I felt like he made an impression on a small group of people. I might be all wrong about this, but what I feel is that he was a big impression on the people he was physically around and knew him. I don't know how big an impression his records had on the people that didn't know him, but I feel pretty sure he was an impression on Sonny Boy Williamson, the first one. I can just tell by the people who were around him, by the respect he got that obviously leads to having an impression on people's music.

So, I think he deserved more recognition than he got. And I think it might have happened if he hadn't been more devoted to raising his family, if he had been a wild man, you know! Had been out touring around and really living it up and being more famous. I don't think he was concerned with that. He was satisfied with who he was, and he knew he was good at what he did, but he didn't need to have adoration by the masses.

I can't doubt that he did have an influence on my playing. I couldn't tell you how. I just believe, if no other way than just the spirit he had toward the music and life. It really left an impression on me, just the way he conducted himself. I really admired the man. The way he carried himself and the way he presented himself and the way his music came across is really impressive. I didn't try to sit down and figure out the things he played, or the way he sang or something. When you're around somebody, you kind of pick up things without thinking about it. I know I was mightily impressed by him and just really generally liked him, and liked hanging out with him. I was really honored that he would go with me to these clubs and things. We had a good time together.

He wasn't rowdy, you know, so there's not any kind of stories like that I can tell. He just was always in a good mood. He would fall asleep sometimes for a few minutes. We'd be in a club. I'd look over; he'd just be, his eyes closed, and he'd be asleep. Then in a few minutes he'd be awake, talkin' and laughing with people. He could go to sleep just about anywhere for just a few minutes and just kind of rejuvenate. I thought that was a pretty remarkable talent. Without slumping over either, he'd just sit there and go right to sleep for a few minutes and then he'd be right back with you.

I could tell all kind of stories about having problems getting paid and getting royalties, so I'm sure Yank had the same trouble. He was smart enough to be aware of those things. My point is he's not a guy with a chip on his shoulder. He had a way with dealin' with things that were. I guess he was a realist, you know, but he didn't carry it on his shoulder. That's probably one of the reasons he didn't devote his life to music, because he knew it was full of so many scammers. One little example on my own side is the first album I made. According to them, it's still in the red. It's been in print for thirty years and it still didn't earn a cent. You wonder why they would keep it in print if it wasn't sellin' any.

Me and Hammie Nixon would hang out together, too. Last time I saw him was in Memphis. I think it was a show out on Mud Island. This was about fifteen years ago. And maybe I saw him again at the Handy Awards.

My influences were more Will Shade and Shakey Horton and Little Walter and Sonny Boy, both Sonny Boys. I liked the first Sonny Boy first. I used to find 78s of his in the junk stores around Memphis. I still love to listen to his playing. Listen to it regularly.

I thought he was a great player, Hammie Nixon; his style sort of reminded me of John Lee Williamson. And maybe that's sort of a West Tennessee, Memphis-area style. There's a guy I knew, he didn't make any records, his name is Clydell Smith; he was from Somerville, Tennessee, and I knew him in Memphis. He kind of played that same sort of style, and there was another guy named Johnny Moman I knew in Memphis, and he kind of played that style a little bit, so probably everybody borrowed something from everybody else and made it a style.

I got the feeling that people borrowed from one another. And it was a real camaraderie between 'em all. Probably there was a lot that went on in West Tennessee that was lost to history, and the only thing that survives today is what was recorded by Yank, Sleepy John, and Sonny Boy. There might have been a lot of Yank Rachells. I don't know.

I remember Homesick James talking about—because he was from around that area—about all these places he used to play. There would be lots of them playing there, these fish fries and country suppers. I remember one story he told about something happened. A big fight broke out and everybody, all the musicians, took off running. And the funny thing was that Sleepy John Estes was the first one to make it back home. When they showed up, Sleepy John was already in bed with the covers pulled over him.

I remember when Sleepy John and Hammie would come up from Brownsville; they would go out from Chicago to play like some of those folk coffeehouses. That's where they were listening to the acoustic blues. And I don't know what happened in New York City; they decided they wanted to leave and they were found hitchhiking in the Holland Tunnel. The police picked them up and drove them to the bus station.

The last time I saw Yank he sang with us at the Slippery Noodle in Indianapolis, and came up on stage. I think he even said something like, I mean he was in a great mood, said something like, "Man, I'm really drunk tonight." We had a really great time. That was about two years ago. I would always call him when I'd come to town, and sometime he'd come down and sometimes he wouldn't, but the last time I was there he was there and got on stage to play with us and sing.

I wish I had been around more, or saw him more, been closer to him. I wanted to have him play on that last album I made for Alligator, but we just didn't have the money. We just ran out of money, you know. And his style of playing, it would really fit with the jug band sound, sort of a Memphis, West Tennessee jug band sound. Well, I'm really gonna miss him.

I really liked his singing a lot, like on "Hobo Blues" and "Thirty-Eight Pistol." He just had a great spirit to him, really just shouting it out. I wish more people had known about him. You couldn't have known a nicer person. A good heart. If the world was made up of people like Yank Rachell, it would be a wonderful place to live.

RY COODER

Ry Cooder is a Warner Brothers recording artist whose musical interests have been uniquely eclectic. He has mixed and matched blues, old-time jazz, country, soul music, rock, stomping Tex-Mex sounds, and anything else that could possibly come to mind. In his hands it's all one thing, really interesting and lively music from all over the world. He has also written the scores for films such as Paris, Texas, *and* Alamo Bay. *Recently, he has had great success with Cuban music. He played on and produced* Buena Vista Social Club, Afro-Cuban All-Stars *(World Circuit/Nonesuch 79476-2) and other albums featuring the veteran Cuban musicians he "rediscovered" in Havana.*

I first heard Sleepy John Estes and Yank Rachell together when they started bringing around traditional players in the sixties and finding whoever was left and who could still play and so forth. And it turned out a lot of them could play very well. It just was another case of nobody had changed much, but the world had sped up and these guys had been left to the dust somehow. I'm thinking of Mississippi John Hurt and Skip James and, of course, Sleepy John.

He showed up at this Ash Grove Club in West Hollywood out here in Los Angeles, and of all the people that I had ever heard on record, the one I was most intrigued with was Sleepy, because I loved his records so much and they really meant a lot to me. I was very much pulled by those records that he made with Yank and Jab Jones [the 1929–30 recording sessions in Memphis]. Out they came, and I was just ecstatic that I was going to get to hear this music. I mean, of all the people, this seemed to be the most remote in time and place to me, and I was in junior high school, maybe fourteen or fifteen, and I thought that this music is coming a distance through time here, and what's left?

But Sleepy John was great. He made two trips out here and I think Yank was on one but not the other. And at some point Hammie Nixon became sort of a fixture with him, and it was never very interesting, but there he was. There Sleepy was, and I began to go see him, as I got older, out in Brownsville, Tennessee. And you could do kind of what was suggested by "going to Brownsville, taking the right-hand road," [the opening lyrics of the song "The Girl I Love, She Got Long Curly Hair"] because the highway takes that T shape there, and if you take that right-hand road you end up with the road petering out in a bean field. Beyond the bean field was his shack where he had lived for a long time. So I used to go out there and give him money, just hand over money to him. And this guy, he was a very strange kind of abstracted individual, and he was just, "Is this for royalties?" I mean, you could have been anybody, you could have been J. P. Morgan or nobody.

But Yank had gone on to Indianapolis. And I remember at that time he seemed to be kind of active. He recorded; he was in folk festivals, but not with Sleepy John. I never found out why that was. I'd go see Sleepy John; it was somewhere in the early 1970s, around the time of the *Boomer's Story* album, before 1975.[1] I could drive out there and check him out. Go to Memphis, rent a car, and drive up. So I was making those records, and you could call Sleepy John and have him come down. Someone would drive him down, record, you know.

As far as the mandolin is concerned, you know I heard Yank's records. I had that record — I think it was Sam Charters who did that one LP, a reissue

---

[1] Ry Cooder's album, *Boomer's Story* (1972, Reprise 9 26398-2). Sleepy John Estes plays on one track, "President Kennedy." Interestingly enough, that track has piano and mandolin on it along with Estes' guitar, the same instrumentation as on the first 1929 recordings by the Three Js.

of all these known tunes. Then a bunch of 'em came out on Swaggie, an Australian collector's label. There were a few that came along. The later sessions from the 1930s weren't as interesting, but they were pretty good. I heard these records and I said, "This is mandolin that I can grasp." I couldn't play bluegrass mandolin worth a damn. It's too hard, and it's much too linear for me. But Yank's style fascinated me because it had a lot of power and it's very raw—and what a great thing to do, just to attack this little instrument like that.

I always ask myself, "Where does this fit in? What's the context for this? Does anybody else do this? Is this a style?" because things are never isolated; they have to exist in some framework. So I started looking around and I found some jug band records. And it may be that it was modeled after a group such as Earl McDonald's Louisville Jug Band, who had a banjo-mandolin player, which is where I think that instrument came from. It's the way these guys used to play that banjo-mandolin. There's no other mandolin players, particularly, who have that kind of stroke and who have that kind of sound that Yank did. But if you use a banjo-mandolin, a little one like they used to make...

It's an instrument that had a banjo head with a mandolin neck on it. It's one of these variants they were producing in those days. That was a popular instrument in these jug bands. They were seen up in Tennessee and in Kentucky, not so much in Memphis jug bands, but a little further north—Earl McDonald's being the one who had, for my money, the greatest player of all time in there, whoever he was. You listen to that guy and you probably understand where Yank is coming from.

At a certain point people stopped playing banjo-mandolins, mainly because they were inferior instruments and the heads would cave in, and these guys wouldn't be able to get the heads replaced. Yank ended up playing mandolin, but black people didn't play mandolins very much. Earlier on, in a time when all these hybrid instruments were being produced, Gibson was making some of them. Like, say, from 1900 to 1925, when they did all of that weird experimenting, the banjo-mandolin was a pretty popular thing. It's loud and had the double strings. It was effective. It would cut through.

I wondered, Where did Sleepy John Estes and Yank Rachell and Jab Jones get this stuff from? This sort of half-time, double-time rhythmic concept, it's very unusual. Sleepy played in half time 'cause that's all he could do. He could barely play. He had a real good rhythmic feel, but he cut everything in half. The piano player played in double time, he sort of kicked it up, and the mandolin goes along and accompanies the voice and duplicates the vocal line. And I thought, that's real interesting, to play in unison with the voice — a kind of style you can't really do on guitar, no one ever does that. Mostly, they don't. Sometimes the bottleneck players would play with themselves; Blind Willie Johnson did that. But in a mandolin it's kind of unusual. Usually the mandolin plays solo, the instrumental breaks. Yank definitely was after playing the melody line while Sleepy John sang these tunes. So he had a nice line. It supports the melody and it kind of fools with the melody; it kind of takes off. It creates interesting rhythmic tension and that was really interesting for me. I thought it was fantastic, how he was able to extract, play with such a sense of urgency.

But you can hear this banjo-mandolin. And when I was younger and I used to listen to those kinds of records, I said to myself, "There's no way that my mandolin sounds like that, and there's no way that my mandolin sounds like Yank Rachell." So I experimented. Sometimes I thought that he tuned his strings funny, that the unison strings weren't unison and one was sharp or flat to the other one; and it may be so 'cause most of these country players didn't tune very well. But when you go to banjo-mandolin, then you begin to get some of that weird — it's got a different sound quality and things begin to make more sense. And I got one, and when I played it, I could get something more of that sound. It also has to do with how you play it. You have to have a certain technique. Maybe Yank, in his early life, played banjo-mandolin and switched to mandolin. I don't know because I never asked him.

That would have been an interesting question, because when people make instrument switches and then stay with the other instrument, they always retain some of the technique that you needed to use on the first one. And that has a lot do with the way people play, because sometimes they learned a certain way on a certain instrument, then they switched and retained some of that technique. Because, God knows, his mandolin technique was idiosyncratic.

Most of rural music is voice centered; the instruments are tuned to the voices. But the upstroke is a lot of where the sound comes from, and I'm sure banjo-mandolin players used the upstroke too, interestingly enough. I don't know why.

It's interesting to listen to some of these jug band records, by groups that are more uptown than Sleepy's group, who are more polished. I always found that what seemed to be happening is the real countrified players, the real rural players were copying something that they heard, like Robert Johnson trying to play like Lonnie Johnson for instance. That's the most obvious example that comes to mind, and Ray Charles trying to sing like Charles Brown. You find that shit all the time. So who in the hell was Sleepy John and Jab Jones and Yank trying to play like? Because Sleepy John learned other people's tunes. He didn't write everything. He would adapt other people's tunes and change some of the lyrics, which he had to, if you were going to record.

Everybody is influenced by who they are around. None of this happens in a vacuum, except that Sleepy John's records were really to me quite unique, until I started to hear some of that other upriver jug band stuff. Then I began to think, "Well, maybe they sought to play in this manner," because jug bands were very popular, you know. You could make money. Earl McDonald was supposed to have been a favorite at the race tracks, up in Louisville, up in Kentucky. Riverboat jobs. They could get work. There's a lot of jug bands, Gus Cannon and all those guys. So it was popular music; you could get work and you needed to be sort of good. And when you started to have more than two people you really needed to be good, because, otherwise, primitive players often can't play with other people. They can't do it because they're so backward, or they're so idiosyncratic that they just can't function in a group setting. But jug bands were invariably three, four, five people.

CONGRESS: Yank described an early band he had with Sleepy John Estes, and it had a tuba, trombone, five or six guys.

COODER: Jesus Christ, that's what I'm saying! And there were some people who could play horns. Anybody in those days who could play horn had to be a little bit better. It's a little harder to play alto saxophone. So, it's really interesting. That means that you were getting into some uptown players who were schooled, and it's hard to think that Sleepy John ever got anywhere near being next to people like that.

But on the other hand, I only saw him when he was an old, broken-down man. But when he was young, he could have been sharp, you know. All those guys could have been sharp. I don't know where they worked. He sings a song about a floating bridge. They had a car. They were going someplace in a car. They had money enough for a car. It's all obscure now. I don't know anything about this shit, except there was a time when there were more instruments used, and most of that stuff never made it to the record date, because I suppose they would give them enough money to bring three people, so you didn't bring your whole band. A damn shame, too. That's really the tragedy of it all.

CONGRESS: Do you feel like you learned some things from Rachell?

COODER: Oh, hell yes! Everything I play on mandolin basically comes from what I was trying to interpret or—it's kind of like, you don't know what's happening, you kind of have to make it up. But when I heard those records, I said, "That's for me! That's what I want to do." So I went out and got a mandolin, a little Gibson A model, and I began to try to play in that manner. Now I didn't like what I did, because I didn't do it right. It was weak. It sounded stringy. It sounded toppy. And I didn't get it. But I kept trying, because it led me into another kind of style of playing mandolin that began to work better for me. But I always stuck with the idea of the mandolin as a blues instrument rather than just strictly as a country instrument—a more polite instrument, a parlor room thing—because I always thought that the mandolin had kind of a, if you played it hard enough and with enough wild abandon, it had a kind of insanity to it that I really liked, a high-pitched sort of screech. Of course, when I saw Yank play, he didn't play like that at all. It was just what was in his hands. And that, of course, is the mystery of being one of those people.

There couldn't be anybody more unlike Yank than me. I'm some white guy from Santa Monica by the sea, in California. And there he is, from down where he is. And so we are completely different as individuals. And you can never be that, and you can never play and get those notes. I don't care how hard you try, and of course it is very hard, it's a very great handling of the instrument.

CONGRESS: Did you talk much to Yank?

COODER: Oh, I think we said hello a couple of times and that would have been about it. There wasn't much to say. I tried to talk to Sleepy John, but it was like talking to a Delphic riddler—kind of the most bizarre conversationalist that I ever met in my life. I spent more time with Sleepy. I wasn't old enough and I wasn't smart enough to ask the right questions and get any answers, I regret to say. Now it would be a different story. But when you are kind of young and just completely unaware of things, you just don't know what is going on. I was just trying to listen and get a handle on things.

PETER ROLLER

Peter Roller is Associate Professor of Music at Alverno College in Milwaukee, Wisconsin. In the 1980s he was a graduate student in musicology at Indiana University and often accompanied Yank Rachell on guitar. He produced the album Blues Mandolin Man, *which was released by Blind Pig Records in 1986. He wrote his master's thesis in musicology on Yank Rachell's musical style.*

On top of doing an oral history, with a lot of quotes from him, including a long pig story, from my field's point of view, I was doing a theoretical take on what is the essence of country blues performing style in a ensemble. Not just the lone guy with a guitar spinning out verses, but Yank's particular tradition, which is always playing in an ensemble, going back to strange jug bands that had horns and mandolins and fiddles.

There is a part of my thesis that is theoretical, that has to do with performance of music like country blues, that is made up of a bunch of choices and a lot of improvisation. How do you manage to pull that off with ensembles of people who don't really know where you are going? Especially in Yank's case, since he was picking up younger accompanists here and there. I plugged into some research that was done on West African music about cueing in drumming ensembles and how a given drum piece can start and go as long as it feels right, and then it's going to have a cue that it's either going to move to something else or it's going to end. And I basically felt, after playing with Yank for a couple of years, that there was a series of cues he used as his way of holding things together, so he can constantly make up lines on the spot—bringing up verses that come to his memory, or even improvising solos on his mandolin and still having people stick with him.

There's some sections in my thesis where I outline that he has these core riffs he plays on his mandolin that kind of keep the cueing happening. There's an ending cue he uses to say the song's over, a descending line of notes. He's got two endings; one's melodic and the other one's a chordal one: da da! da da! da da da da DA! And not everyone has that, so to me that was clearly an ending cue. He also has intro cues, because he plays in two keys. He plays in E or he plays in A. And he just plays these little riffs and he looks you in the eye and he sees if you know what key you are supposed to play in. That's the theoretical side; and there are some transcriptions of the melodies that he plays.

There's a final point. All this serves his ability to improvise and play his mandolin, which ultimately serve him showing off his individuality. The title of my thesis was about individualism, and that's what I thought with Yank. It was all about "I play my blues on the mandolin, and I'm the only guy who's really done it this way."

I guess it's important to say Yank was such a warm person, that we were very close. He was hurt that I had to move away to take my first job out of grad school. We kept in touch, and I drove up from Florida when he went to play at Blind Willie's in Atlanta, and hang out with him and also play with him at least once. That was one of the only clubs outside of Indy that he would go to once and a while. That was about 1986 and 1987. Yank would jump into a car with Sheena, and maybe with someone else; and Eric King, who ran Blind Willie's, would put him up. He was hip enough to know Yank was special. It was interesting because Atlanta has such a big black middle-class scene and there was a more racially mixed audience. When he walked into the club once, a kid said, "There's Blind Willie!"

Yank had a great capacity to love other people. Numerous times he said to folklorists, "I don't care if you are young, old, black, red, yellow, white, or green. If you can play some blues, then I want to hear from ya." And I became a part of his household sort of. He came to Milwaukee and played up here as a sign of friendship after I moved my job up here. He took a gig up here with Sheena and had a really great gig at the Wisconsin Conservatory of Music, where I had my first job. It was in this formal recital hall in an old mansion. Yank and I did it as a duo, and later on we went over to the main blues bar and played with this typical electric blues ensemble, and had a big time for a weekend.

Country blues is more flexible than urban blues, which keeps to a set twelve-bar pattern. That's what Charles Keil says in *Urban Blues*. And in my thesis I say that when Yank plays the kind of blues that he plays, he has to play with people who are able to play thirteen-and-a-half-bar blues. Some old tunes are eleven and a half bars long, but they are regular. That's sort of my thesis: the heart of what he's playing is country blues, even though he's playing electric mandolin, and he had such a strong emphasis on doing his own thing.

I've seen Yank throw off many an accompanist, including African Americans. One guy, a black bass player, just shouted to him during a gig or rehearsal. He said, "You ain't playin' the right blues! You ain't playin' twelve bars!" as if Yank had done something wrong.

Yank had a whole lot of blues stanzas in his memory, but he would improvise by just picking out which ones he wanted on the spot. He had basically tune families. You run into this in David Evans' *Big Road Blues*. As long as certain verses fit into tune families, they'll just mix and match them. It's improvisation.

DAVID "HONEYBOY" EDWARDS

"Honeyboy" Edwards, born in Shaw, Mississippi, in 1915, now lives in Chicago. His first recordings were made for the Library of Congress in 1942 in Clarksdale, Mississippi, by Alan Lomax. In 1997 his autobiography, The World Don't Owe Me Nothing, *was published by Chicago Review Press. He is still musically active.*

I knowed Yank right in that time, '35, '36, when I played with the Memphis Jug Band. We used to come in the park in Memphis and play some. Most all musicians from Arkansas and Mississippi would come in the park on Friday and Saturday and play. That was the only place to go. There was a big park and the people be walkin' the streets. They come from Arkansas and way down there in Mississippi and go on Beale Street, and they'd go out where the blues was bein' played. And we were drinkin' and doin' everything out there. Yeah, they'd give us a nickel and dime, quarter, make us a little money, you know. That's where the best blues was at; that's were the big crowd would be.

I never recorded with Yank, but Joe Williams did, and Sleepy John; they worked together for a good while. Yank knowed a lot of friends.

I never did play mandolin. I tried to play violin a little bit, and I recorded with harp a lot, with the rack and guitar. It was pretty close together, my style of blues and Yank's. But I had a little different style. But the blues is the blues. You know what I mean? Everybody got a little something in their stuff another don't have, just about. But Yank was a good musician, playin' the blues, and they had that Tennessee style. He come up with John Estes and Son Bonds. He played a lot with Son Bonds and Hammie Nixon—he blow the jug.

Every once in a while I would see Yank in the '50s and '60s. And when Yank lived in St. Louis, we always got together. Then Yank disappeared from St. Louis; he went down to Brownsville where his family was. I lived in St. Louis a year or so, and then I went down to Brownsville, where Yank was livin'. And I was inquiring about him and I found where he lived at. He lived over in a big old house in the pasture, like about a six-, seven-room house. All the kids was small then. Yank had moved back from St. Louis. And him and Big Joe, they were workin' together then, and Jimmy Joe Shaw—he was my cousin, supposed to be. So I left St. Louis and went down south and went different places. Then I heard that Yank had moved to Indianapolis, and he went to work in some kind of mill. Then I always knowed where Yank was, and every once in a while we'd run up on each other. I been knowin' Yank a long time.

Well, you take Sleepy John and Yank, they had a lot of the old style of playing, you know what I mean? You take Sleepy John, he played the older style of blues, that old C and G blues, you know what I mean? And Yank play lots in A too, after Yank start recordin'. You know, A is the best blues key you can play in and E is the best blues key you can play in, just about. Most any blues player, guitar player, he play A and G blues. Lonnie Johnson and Big Bill Broonzy was about the only two guitar players I knowed that played a lot of blues in C. But you take like Tampa Red, he played in all kind of keys, Spanish, Vastapol, you know. Spanish and Vastapol mean you play a lot of it in slide, slide guitar. Big Bill, he never played nothin' like that, but Big Bill really was a good finger man, and Lonnie Johnson. They liked the key of C; they were C men! But most of the later style of blues players, they play A blues and E. B. B. King play a lot in A and some in C, but not too much in C.

I liked Yank's style. Yank was a good blues player. He was a good vocalist, he sung good too. I like that, a lot of his old songs like "Diving Duck." Yeah, I knowed Yank a long time.

HOWARD "LOUIE BLUIE" ARMSTRONG

Howard Armstrong was born in Dayton, Tennessee, in 1909. At an early age he learned to play violin, mandolin, and guitar. A veteran string band musician, he has played all over the world. His musical style is eclectic to an extreme. He is also a painter and accomplished storyteller.

I had been playin' on festivals and things with Yank, not exactly with him, but on the same bill. We were nice friends, you know, and several years ago he was in a documentary, *Louie Bluie* [a film made by Terry Zwigoff about Armstrong's life]. That was around '84 or '85. I heard him play many times. I thought he was a very wonderful musician. He played the mandolin all the time, and he played usually with his own accompaniment. Yes, I think the first time I heard him play was up at Wolf Trap. I knew Sleepy John Estes and Hammie Nixon too.

I was interested in guys that played mandolin. He played a pretty different style from most mandolin players, 'cause it seems that most black musicians don't play mandolin much anymore, you know what I mean? See, now you find many, many men like B. B. King and those guys who play electric guitar, but not mandolin. That's one thing that attracted me to him. He was a good mandolin player.

All that I remember that Yank played, he was definitely a blues player, a blues man. That's what he played. Course I play a conglomerate of just about everything, including ethnic songs.

I know a few lines of some of the blues songs, well one of 'em that he used to play and sing: "If the ocean was whiskey and I was a divin' duck, I'd dive to the bottom and I wouldn't come up." Things like that. He was a mandolin blues player, and one time I remember his granddaughter played the bass with him. I met her two or three times at the festivals.

Well, I don't know much about his personal habits, if he drink whiskey. I never had a drink in my life and never smoked a cigarette. Oh yeah, I considered him one of my best friends, musical friends. I don't know much about his home life or nothin' like that. I only met him on the road; we'd stay at the same hotel.

When they made that movie, Yank and I would take a break and pass the time. We sittin' around, you know, at the lodge where we'd be staying, teasin' each other, you know. As a matter of fact I'm gonna tell ya something. This guy Terry Zwigoff, who filmed the thing—a lot of things I would not have said in the movie if I'd of known he was doing that. He would kind of creep up on us settin' around chewing the fat, you know, lettin' our hair down, using all kind of language that I wouldn't do it in real nice society. And he just put it all down on tape.

DORIS JOHNSON

At the time of this interview (1997) Doris Johnson was the executive director of the Indiana Blues Society.

The main mission of the Blues Society is to promote, perpetuate the blues and blues musicians in the state of Indiana. We do all kinds of events, festivals, bring in national headliners. We have a blues-in-the-schools program, a fund that we use to have an education co-coordinator, Charlie Edmonds, go out to the schools. He teaches about the history of the blues and does some performing, and we also subsidize the cost for an artist to go and perform for the students in schools that are too poor to pay for it themselves. We teach them the history of the blues.

I met Yank in 1983, just through the blues scene. I started following him pretty extensive whenever he played. He always had a great crowd around him all the time. I got to be pretty good friends with him, had him over to the house a number of times for dinner. Then I found he was not getting booked properly. He just didn't have anybody doing anything or getting him any gigs. People around here would consider him a local band and bar owners would want to pay him local wages—two, three hundred dollars. So he asked if there was any way I could help him get any other bookings besides the local ones; this was back in '92. I kind of started a little booking agency called Blues Net Productions. Yank was really the only person I booked for; and the first gig we got him was opening for Buddy Guy and B. B. King at the Deer Creek music center in Nobelsville. It's our largest outdoor amphitheater. I booked him at several festivals the next couple of years, where he could get better pay, such as a thousand dollars or fifteen hundred dollars. I booked him at out-of-state gigs, the Garvin Gate Blues Festival at Louisville, Kentucky, and the Mississippi Valley Blues Festival in Davenport, Iowa.

We'd always book him at our festivals. We always paid him well, upwards of a thousand dollars. I always said Yank was not a local band, even though he lived in Indianapolis. He was an international star. We always tried to portray that to anyone who wanted to book him. We really backed him on that.

The Blues Society tried to do as much as it could. We had an annual birthday party for Yank for the last eleven years. Actually, the Blues Society anniversary was in March also, so we had the Blues Society of Indiana–Yank Rachell Birthday Bash every year with proceeds going to Yank. Everyone brought him presents; he just loved that. Our main goal was just to get him out there and get him paid well. I booked him also at the Chicago Blues Festival and the St. Louis Jazz Heritage Festival their first year of that. He played there with Henry Townsend. That was around '93.

This year [1997] there was the big event on January 25 with John Sebastian. So, we gave him cash at that event. That was one of the specialest things I've seen for Yank. The place only holds 250 people and there were 300. I got him hooked up with the Red Cross. We got him a wheelchair; we got him an air conditioner, got him a stove—worked with Bruce Iglauer of Alligator Records—those kind of things that he couldn't afford. One of the goals of the Blues Society was to just try to take care of him.

That event in January was probably the best I've ever seen Yank play and look. He was in his wheelchair, but he still could get up and move around. It was a good day. It was funny; we got a wheelchair for him through Medicare. I asked him how it was and he said, "Oh, it's great, I use it around the house." I asked, "Don't you take it out?" He had to go to the hospital a couple times a week. And he went, "Oh no, I'm not going to mess it up. I'm not taking it outside." "That's what it's for. The insurance will replace it anyway." He was kind of a character.

People would offer two or three hundred dollars for him to travel somewhere and he'd pretty much say, "Yeah, yeah, I'll be there." He'd wait until the last minute and say, "I couldn't leave my backyard for less than a thousand dollars." He'd feel like if they were cheap enough to offer him those kind of prices he would let on like he'd be there and then he'd just not go. It used to piss off those who were trying to get him there for so little. You gotta consider that a payback. I always thought that was kind of great. You wouldn't believe the kind of argument we'd have. People would say, "Well, he hasn't done much," just because they didn't know his history, and they would want to offer him so little to come somewhere.

Yank was a womanizer to the end. I booked him at the St. Louis Jazz Heritage Festival one year, and I went up to his room and was hanging out. He must have been eighty-four or eighty-five, and he cornered me in the room, "Just give me a kiss, just give me a kiss."

"Yank, I can't do that."

"It's because I'm black, isn't it?"

"No, it's because you're fifty years older than I am. You're old enough to be my grandfather."

"Well, haven't you heard, 'The older the buck the stiffer the horn'?"

That's one of my great little stories about Yank. I said, "Yank, I can't believe you're still chasing women at eighty-five, eighty-seven years old."

And he said, "Well, I'm not dead yet." He was just really with it. Not what you think of as your normal senior citizen.

Once he got out of Indy to play festivals he started getting calls for booking. People were amazed at his age and that he was still an active musician. He got thirty years younger when he played. It just perked him up so much.

He was almost impossible when he was getting ready for a concert. His shoes had to match his socks and his hat. He was just impeccable when it came to dressing: "I can't wear that suit. I don't have a hat that matches it." He was real picky.

Dave Morgan

Dave Morgan is a music teacher and blues performer in Indianapolis. He produced and accompanied Rachell on the 1995 Slippery Noodle Sound CD, Pig Trader Blues. *Morgan begins by talking about touring with Rachell in Indiana.*

We were driving in Crawfordsville and, as you know, it's a very white community and very affluent. All these well-dressed people were walking in downtown Crawfordsville. We were going to this very nice place to play, and Yank is looking all around, and I knew what's going to come out of his mouth. He says, "Ain't no black people here, are there?" I said, "Not that I know of Yank, not that many." He says, "They got one now, so they best get used to it." And by the time we left Crawfordsville, the guy could have had anything in Crawfordsville he wanted, in just hours. So he was kind of astounding that way in his ability to touch individuals. Everyone just loved the guy. He was a very warm guy. But when his wife died he had a chance to make a lot of money. He had a lot of personality and charisma. But with his wife gone he had the kids and grandkids to take care of.

He was the master of one-liners. He loved doing the dozens, verbally cutting on me. He liked to do it because I would play along, just take it so he could get a laugh out of the audience. One night he started talking about who was the ugliest on the stage. I got in a pretty good retort about how he reminded me of a beauty contest in my hometown where nobody won. So he came back with, "Well, you're so damn ugly you make an onion cry."

One night he was gettin' all over the drummer. The drummer was playing too hard. Then he just stopped in the middle of the song and turned to the drummer and said, "Damn it boy! I told you to drive those drums, not wreck 'em!" We were his straight men. Everyone loved it. He would say, "They like that. I'm a lot older than you and you're a white boy and I'm a black man. They like to see us there playin' like that."

I'd get him up from dialysis and go on a gig. He'd sleep on the way, then eat something and he was rarin' to go. He'd put on a three-hour show. I don't know how he did it. Just, probably, growing up real tough as a young man.

Offers came in all the time for him to travel for concerts and festivals in the U.S. and Europe. But he couldn't travel. He was afraid to go overseas because he didn't want to die there. The offers would have snowballed if he had been able to do festivals and concerts, because he was so good with crowds. He would go into a club that seated fifty, and there would be two hundred there. And he'd take half an hour to get to the stage because Yank would shake hands and have a conversation with everyone.

Appendix 4

Musicians

The following is a listing of the musicians and music business people mentioned by Yank. The biographical information is by necessity brief. The main sources used were *Blues Who's Who* by Sheldon Harris, *The Big Book of Blues* by Robert Santelli, and *The Encyclopedia of the Blues* by Gérard Herzhaft. There are several individuals Yank mentioned about whom nothing further can be ascertained. Of the many southern rural musicians of his time, only the fortunate few were in the right place at the right time to be recorded or documented.

Adams, J. T.: John Tyler Adams was born in Morganfield, Kentucky, in 1911 and died, place unknown (most likely Indianapolis), sometime in the 1970s. A guitarist who moved to Indianapolis in 1941, he mostly worked outside music. He played local clubs and house parties with Scrapper Blackwell, Shirley Griffith, Yank Rachell, and others. He recorded on the Bluesville label with Griffith in Indianapolis in 1961.

Barbee, John Henry: William George Tucker was born in Henning, Tennessee, in 1905 and died in Chicago, Illinois, in 1964. He played guitar and worked with Sonny Boy Williamson and Sunnyland Slim, among others, in Tennessee, Mississippi, and Arkansas. In 1938 he recorded in Chicago. He changed his name after leaving Arkansas over a shooting. During the 1960s he toured and recorded.

Bates, Leroy: Also known as Lefty Bates, he was a guitarist who lived in Indianapolis and played with Yank Rachell. He made a few recordings in Chicago between 1955 and 1960.

Blackwell, Scrapper: Francis Hillman Blackwell was born in Syracuse, South Carolina, in 1903 and died in Indianapolis, Indiana. A guitarist, he moved to Indianapolis as a child. There he teamed with pianist Leroy Carr, and they recorded in 1928. They also worked together in clubs locally and in St. Louis. After Carr died in 1935, Blackwell played infrequently. He recorded for the 77, Bluesville, and other labels between 1958 and 1961. He was shot to death in 1962.

Bloomfield, Mike: Michael Bernard Bloomfield was born in Chicago, Illinois, in 1943 and died in San Francisco, California, in 1981. He played guitar, harmonica, and piano. In 1962 he began working clubs in Chicago and played with Big Joe Williams and other older bluesmen. He toured and recorded with the Paul Butterfield Blues Band and on his own. He was highly regarded as a blues guitarist. He died of a drug overdose.

Bonds, Son: He was born in Brownsville, Tennessee, in 1909 and died in Dyersburg, Tennessee, in 1947. He lived and worked in the Brownsville area. A guitar player, he worked with Hammie Nixon and Sleepy John Estes. He recorded with Nixon in 1934 and with Estes in 1939 and 1941. Bonds was sitting on a front porch when he was shot and killed. The murderer was a jealous lover who mistook Bonds for someone else.

Bonham, Gordon: An Indiana blues musician who played with Yank Rachell, he has also worked with bluesmen Jimmy Walker and Gary Primich.

Brim, John: He was born in Hopkinsville, Kentucky, in 1922. A guitarist and harmonica player, he lived in Indianapolis in the early 1940s and then moved to Chicago. He played with Sonny Boy Williamson, Jimmy Reed, and Big

Maceo. He first recorded in 1950. He lives in Gary, Indiana, and records for the Tone Cool label.

Brindle, Beki: A singer and guitarist who played extensively with Yank Rachell in Indianapolis during the 1990s, she has performed with Jerry Lee Lewis among other notable musicians.

Broonzy, Big Bill: William Lee Conley Broonzy was born in Scott, Mississippi, in 1893 and died in Chicago, Illinois, in 1958. Both of his parents were born into slavery. Famous as a guitarist and singer, he started out playing the fiddle in church and for country parties. He was an itinerant preacher and then served in the army in World War I. Relocating to Chicago in 1920, he eventually recorded with many blues singers, starting in 1927. A popular musician in Chicago, he helped many artists (including Muddy Waters) get a start. He played clubs, concerts, and many world tours until he became too ill in 1957. Starting out as a rough country performer, he incorporated urban and jazz-influenced sounds into his music. When he toured Europe he presented himself as more of a down-home folk musician. He wrote an autobiography with Yannick Bruynoghe, *Big Bill Blues*, that was published in 1955 by Cassell and Company, Ltd.

Brown, Lee: From Ripley, Tennessee, he was a piano player who first recorded with Sleepy John Estes and Hammie Nixon in 1937. His song "Little Girl, Little Girl" was popular, and he recorded for a number of years.

Butterfield, Paul: He was born in Chicago, Illinois, in 1942 and died in North Hollywood, California, in 1987. He played harmonica and sang. He worked clubs in Chicago and formed the Butterfield Blues Band in the mid-1960s. He recorded and toured with his band, which found an audience among rock and roll fans. He died of a drug and alcohol overdose.

Calloway, Cab: He was born in Rochester, New York, in 1907 and died in 1994. A flashy big band leader and showman who was very popular in the swing era, he came to national prominence leading a band at the Cotton Club in Harlem in the 1930s. He had many hit records and toured with his band through the 1940s. In later life he appeared in theater and film. Sometimes called the "Hi-De-Ho Man," his best-known song is "Minnie the Moocher." His sister, Blanche Calloway, was a prominent blues and jazz singer and recording artist in the 1920s and 1930s.

Cannon, Gus: He was born in Red Banks, Mississippi, in 1883 and died in Memphis, Tennessee, in 1979. He played banjo, guitar, fiddle, jug, and piano. He entertained at sawmills, levee camps, and plantations in the south. In the 1920s he formed Cannon's Jug Stompers. He recorded for Paramount in Chicago in 1927. From 1928 to 1930 he recorded on Victor (in Memphis) and Brunswick (in Chicago). He recorded for Folkways in 1956 and Stax in 1963 (both times in Memphis). He also appeared in a documentary film, *The Blues*, in 1963, and a PBS-TV production, *Good Mornin' Blues*, in 1978. He continued playing music, occasionally working outside music, into the 1960s.

Carr, Leroy: He was born in Nashville, Tennessee, in 1905 and died in Indianapolis, Indiana, in 1935. A piano player, he teamed up with guitarist Scrapper Blackwell in 1928, and they recorded and toured together until Carr died of acute alcoholism. Their piano-guitar duets played an important role in creating an urban blues sound distinct from country blues.

Cotten, Elizabeth: She was born in Chapel Hill, North Carolina, in 1893 and died in Syracuse, New York, in 1987. A self-taught guitar and banjo player and singer, she worked most of her life outside of music. Only as an older adult did she become a public performer. She played at the Newport Folk Festival in 1964 and began recording and touring. She had a traditional, old-time music sound.

Crawford, Pete: A guitar player who worked with Jimmy Walker in Chicago, he also recorded with Yank Rachell on the Delmark CD, *Chicago Style*. He is currently a restaurant owner in Chicago.

DeMyer, Larry: He is an Indianapolis guitarist and producer who played extensively with Yank Rachell in the 1990s.

Edwards, David "Honeyboy:" Born in Shaw, Mississippi, in 1915, he now lives in Chicago. He sings and plays guitar and harmonica. He worked parties and dances in the South with Big Joe Williams and later with Tommy McClennan. He played with Charlie Patton in the Mississippi Delta. In 1934 he went to Memphis and played in the Memphis Jug Band and later worked with Robert Johnson in Mississippi. His first recordings were made for the Library of Congress in 1942 in Clarksdale, Mississippi, by Alan Lomax. Edwards went to Chicago in the 1940s and worked clubs, recorded commercially, and later toured nationally and in Europe. He is still active in music. In 1997 his autobiography, *The World Don't Owe Me Nothing*, was published by Chicago Review Press.

Estes, Sleepy John: John Adam Estes was born in Ripley, Tennessee, in 1899, according to the *Blues Who's Who*, but other sources cite 1904 as his birth date. He died in Brownsville, Tennessee, in 1977. He suffered an eye injury as a child and went blind later in life. His propensity to take naps earned him the name "Sleepy." He began playing local house parties and clubs with Yank Rachell in the 1920s and 1930s. He also worked extensively with Hammie Nixon. He recorded, played festivals, and toured Europe and Japan in the 1960s and 1970s following his rediscovery in 1962. He had a compelling, high, plaintive singing voice and was a strikingly original composer of songs.

Franklin, Pete: Edward Lamonte Franklin was born in Indianapolis, Indiana, in 1928 and died there in 1975. He played guitar and piano. While in the army he was assigned to work as an entertainer. He first recorded in 1947 for Victor in Chicago. He recorded for Bluesville in 1961 and worked local club and house party dates and also performed at the Folk Festival at Wolf Trap in Vienna, Virginia, in 1971.

Gary, Tommy: Harmonica player from the Brownsville area and an influence on Hammie Nixon, he recorded with Sleepy John Estes for Adelphi in Memphis in 1969 and 1970.

Griffith, Shirley: He was born in Brandon, Mississippi, in 1908 and died in Indianapolis, Indiana, in 1974. He learned to play guitar from Tommy Johnson in Mississippi. He moved to Indianapolis in 1928 and played with Scrapper Blackwell for house parties and local clubs. He recorded for Bluesville in 1961. In 1968 he toured the East Coast with Yank Rachell. He also played various blues festivals.

Hooker, John Lee: Born in Clarksdale, Mississippi, in 1917, he left home for Memphis, where he played guitar on street corners. He worked outside of music in Cincinnati and Detroit. In 1948 in Detroit he recorded "Boogie Chillen," which became his signature song. Hooker also recorded a version of Yank Rachell's "Hobo Blues" in 1949. He has toured and recorded extensively and has been a big influence on rock musicians. He has recorded with many of them, including Eric Clapton. He lives in Los Angeles.

Jackson, Jim: He was born in Hernando, Mississippi, in 1890 and died there in 1937. He was a guitar player and singer who worked in minstrel and medicine shows throughout the South. In Memphis he worked with Will Shade and Gus Cannon. He recorded on Victor and Vocalion in the 1920s. He was known as a good entertainer, and his most popular song was "Kansas City Blues."

Jefferson, Lemon: Blind Lemon Jefferson was born in Couchman, Texas, in 1893 and died in Chicago, Illinois. Born blind on a farm, he sang on the streets for tips, in barrelhouses, and at parties and brothels in several Texas cities. He worked in medicine shows and recorded for Paramount from 1926 to 1929. A very important early blues guitarist and singer, his records were extremely popular. In December 1929 he was found dead on a Chicago street during a blizzard.

Johnson, Stormy: A drummer from Indianapolis, he frequently played in Yank Rachell's bands.

Jones, Jab: He played piano on the 1929 recordings with Yank Rachell and Sleepy John Estes. In 1932 he recorded with the Picaninny Jug Band. He also recorded with the Memphis Jug Band in 1934.

Kid Spoon(s): He often performed spoons with jug bands in Memphis in the 1930s and recorded with Robert Wilkins, Minnie Wallace, and Son Joe in 1935. His real name is not known.

King, B. B.: Riley B. King was born in Indianola, Mississippi, in 1925. He is the best known bluesman worldwide. As a child he sang in church, learned guitar, and later worked on a plantation. He moved to Memphis as a young man and played guitar and sang on the streets. He first recorded in 1949 and hosted a radio program on WDIA. The "B. B." came from an early performing name of "Blues Boy." He has toured, recorded, and appeared on TV and in films numerous times and won many music awards. In spite of his commercial success, he has remained true to a "deep blues" sound.

Koester, Robert: He is the owner of an independent jazz and blues label, Delmark Records, and the Jazz Record Mart in Chicago. Sleepy John Estes was thought to be dead for many years when Robert Koester got word that a documentary filmmaker had seen him in Brownsville, Tennessee. Koester immediately located him, and then Hammie Nixon, who had Rachell's address in Indianapolis. Koester arranged for them to record and tour together.

Lewis, Ham: Hambone Lewis played the jug and was sometimes a member of the Memphis Jug Band. No other biographical material was found.

Lewis, Noah: He was born in Henning, Tennessee, in 1895 and died in Ripley, Tennessee, in 1961. A harmonica player, he performed on the streets and for parties before World War I. He worked and recorded with Gus Cannon's Jug Stompers in the 1920s and 1930s. Lewis played an important role in the development of the harmonica as a blues instrument.

Lippman, Horst: A German blues enthusiast, he, together with Fritz Rau, organized the American Folk Blues Festival, which brought blues musicians from the United States to tour western Europe in 1962. It was successful enough to be repeated annually until 1972.

Mahal, Taj: Henry Saint Claire Fredricks was born in New York City in 1942 of West Indian parents; he was raised in Springfield, Massachusetts. He moved to Los Angeles, California, and worked with Ry Cooder. He has recorded and toured extensively. An eclectic talent, he has recorded albums of traditional country blues, urban blues, reggae, and combinations of different musical styles. He has also made film soundtracks.

Melrose, Lester: The famous A&R (artist and repertoire) man for Bluebird Records, he was born in Olney, Illinois, in 1891 and died in Florida in 1968. A producer, talent scout, and publisher, he presided over the recordings of many important blues musicians. He also worked for Vocalion and Okeh.

Memphis Jug Band: Started by Will Shade in the mid-1920s, it was one of the most popular jug bands during the late 1920s and early 1930s, when jug band music was all the rage. Many fine musicians passed through its ranks, including Furry Lewis, Big Walter Horton, and Charlie Burse. Shade signed a recording contract with Victor in 1927 and recorded nearly sixty songs for the label. In contrast to the often heavy and sorrowful Mississippi Delta blues, Shade's jug band created a lighter, upbeat, good-time sound. Its repertoire was a mixture of blues, jazz, ragtime, and popular music, all delivered with a showman's panache.

Memphis Minnie: Lizzie Douglas was born in Algiers, Louisiana, in 1897 and died in Memphis, Tennessee, in 1973. One of the first female blues singers to play guitar on records, she made her first recording in 1929. She performed, toured, and recorded into the mid-1950s.

Montgomery, Little Brother: Eurreal Wilford Montgomery was born in Kentwood, Louisiana, in 1906 and died in Chicago, Illinois, in 1985. A versatile piano player who created a style that drew from New Orleans jazz and barrelhouse piano, he played blues and boogie woogie. He spent most of the 1930s in Jackson, Mississippi, and later moved to Chicago. He recorded, played festivals, and toured Europe. One of his most influential songs was "Vicksburg Blues."

Montgomery, Wes: John Leslie Montgomery was born in Indianapolis, Indiana, in 1925 and died there in 1968. He was a self-taught jazz guitar player who began his national career touring with Lionel Hampton from 1948 through 1950. He formed a group with his two brothers, and they recorded together. He had a distinctive style that featured playing in octaves and a soft sound that came from picking with his thumb instead of a plectrum. He made several recordings with well-known jazz musicians and then later found appeal with a wider audience through a series of highly orchestrated albums that featured popular tunes such as "Tequila," "California Dreaming," and Beatles' songs.

Morgan, Dave: Born in Indianapolis, Indiana, in 1949, he is an Indianapolis blues guitarist and singer who produced and performed with Yank Rachell on the *Pig Trader Blues* CD. He teaches an acoustic blues class at Indiana University–Purdue University, Indianapolis.

Musselwhite, Charlie: Charles Douglas Musselwhite was born in Kosciusko, Mississippi, in 1944. He primarily plays harmonica, but also guitar. His father was a musician and mandolin maker; his mother was a Choctaw Indian. As a teenager he played at local clubs in Chicago with many black bluesmen, including Yank Rachell, Homesick James, Johnny Young, and Robert Nighthawk. He recorded his first album in 1968. He has recorded often and toured widely, playing festivals and clubs.

Newbern, Willie: He was known as Hambone Willie Newbern. An early version of "Roll and Tumble Blues" was recorded by Newbern in 1929. It influenced later recordings by Robert Johnson, Muddy Waters, and others. Over the years "Roll and Tumble" became a southern blues standard. Its melody appeared in the songs of Sleepy John Estes and probably reflects a local blues style rooted in the rural towns of western Tennessee near Memphis.

Peer, Ralph: In 1928, while working for Victor Records, he established the Southern Music Publishing Company. He went to Memphis to set up a field unit to record blues singers and other artists who worked in the area. He recorded many performers, known and unknown, including white country singer Jimmie Rodgers, Fats Waller, and Jelly Roll Morton.

Pickett, Charlie: A guitarist and singer from Brownsville, Tennessee, little else is known about him. He recorded only four songs, all in 1937.

Redbeans and Rice: An Indianapolis-based band that often backed up Yank in public performances during the 1990s. Consisting of Yun Hui Percifield on keyboard and vocals, Bill Young on drums, Jeff Triwedi on saxophone and guitar, and Tom Beckelhimer on bass, they play blues, jazz, and fusion.

Rush, Otis: Born in Philadelphia, Mississippi, in 1934, a singer and guitar player, he moved to Chicago at an early age and played the local clubs. He began recording in 1956 and has done extensive touring. He worked with T-Bone Walker and Little Richard.

Sebastian, John: A recording artist who was part of the popular 1960s singing group The Loving Spoonful, he has an interest in traditional music and has made recent recordings with his jug band.

Shade, Will: Also known as Son Brimmer, he was born in Memphis, Tennessee, in 1898 and died there in 1966. He sang and played guitar, harmonica, jug, and bass. He was with the Furry Lewis Jug Band in Memphis in 1917. In the

1920s he was part of the Memphis Jug Band along with Jab Jones and Ham Lewis. Beginning in 1927 he recorded for Victor.

Smith, Bessie: She was born in Chattanooga, Tennesse, in 1894 and died in Clarksdale, Mississippi, in 1937. Her parents died when she was eight, and she sang on the street for pennies. She toured the South singing in tent shows. Recording frequently for Columbia Records beginning in 1923, she was one of the early "Blues Divas" who helped popularize blues singing.

Spann, Otis: He was born in Jackson Mississippi, in 1930 and died in Chicago, Illinois, in 1970. He worked outside of music and played local clubs in Jackson. He became a professional boxer and later served in the army. He recorded and toured regularly with the Muddy Waters band in Chicago in the 1950s, and he played many music festivals in the 1960s and was known for a strong Chicago blues sound. He died of cancer.

St. Louis Jimmy: James Burke Oden was born in Nashville, Tennessee, in 1903 and died in Chicago, Illinios, in 1977. A piano player who moved to St. Louis as a teenager, he worked house parties and local clubs, frequently playing with Big Joe Williams. He first recorded for Bluebird in 1933. Together with Memphis Minnie he owned a blues club in Indianapolis during the 1940s. He recorded with Muddy Waters and lived with Muddy Waters' family in Chicago in the late 1950s into the 1960s.

Stratyner, Allen: Born in New York City in 1950, he is an Indianapolis harmonica player who played and recorded with Yank Rachell. He teaches harmonica at Indiana University–Purdue University, Indianapolis, and played on Rachell's last CD, *Too Hot for the Devil.*

Sunnyland Slim: Albert Luandrew was born in Vance, Mississippi, in 1907 and died in Chicago, Illinois, in 1995. He played organ and piano and hoboed through the South playing juke joints and parties. He lived in Memphis, and later Chicago, and worked with Tampa Red, Sonny Boy Williamson (the second one), and Muddy Waters, first recording in 1946.

Tampa Red: Hudson Whittaker was born in Smithville, Georgia, in 1904 and died in Chicago, Illinois, in 1981. Tampa Red was raised in Tampa, Florida; he played guitar, piano, and kazoo and played music in clubs around the state. In 1925 he moved to Chicago and recorded first in 1928. Ma Rainey and Georgia Tom were performers he often accompanied. Well regarded as an original songwriter and accomplished musician, he played extensively in the Chicago area until health problems made him less active in the mid 1950s.

Townsend Henry: Born in Shelby, Mississippi, in 1909, he first recorded in 1929. He settled in St. Louis and worked often with John Lee Williamson (the first Sonny Boy), Aleck "Rice" Miller (Sonny Boy number two), Robert Nighthawk, Roosevelt Sykes, and Walter Davis. He has recorded often and played at music festivals since the 1960s. His autobiography, *A Life in the Blues* (University of Illinois Press), was published at the end of 1999.

Turner, Big Joe: Joseph Vernon Turner was born in Kansas City, Missouri, in 1911 and died in Inglewood, California, in 1985. He sang, toured, and recorded with Benny Moten, Count Basie, Harry James, and other big bands. A popular entertainer, he became known as "the boss of the blues." With the decline of big bands in the 1950s, he made a transition to rhythm and blues and later crossed over into early rock and roll.

Walker, Jimmy: He was born in Memphis, Tennessee, in 1905 and died in Chicago, Illinois, in 1998. He moved to Chicago as a child and learned piano. He played with Homesick James and Big Joe Williams. He recorded on the Testament label in 1964 and subsequently played many music festivals.

Wallace, Sippie: Beulah Wallace was born in Houston, Texas, in 1898 and died in Detroit, Michigan, in 1986. Playing piano and organ, she worked in tent shows from her late teens into the 1920s. She recorded in 1923 on the Okeh label. She also recorded with jazz pioneer King Oliver. She devoted a lot of time to gospel music and church work. During the folk revival of the 1960s she returned to blues singing and played music festivals and toured.

Waters, Muddy: McKinley Morganfield was born in Rolling Fork, Mississippi, in 1915 and died in Westmont, Illinois, in 1983. A guitar and harmonica player, he worked as a farmer in the 1920s and 1930s and played music on the side. He was recorded by a Library of Congress field team in 1941 and 1942. He moved to Chicago in 1943. His first commercial recording was in 1947. His dynamic, ensemble style of playing transformed the blues and directly influenced rock musicians such as Eric Clapton and the Rolling Stones. He played and recorded extensively into the 1980s, touring the world and appearing in films and videos.

Webb, Pat: Born in Springfield, Missouri, in 1932, as a youngster he led blind musicians to play on the street corner or at parties. He was a "lead boy" for Blind Tommy Hunt and learned to play the blues from him. He traveled extensively in the 1960s and 1970s, recording and performing. When he lived in Indianapolis in the 1980s and 1990s he frequently played guitar with Yank Rachell and produced his last CD, *Too Hot for the Devil.* Webb now lives in Nashville, Indiana.

Williams, Big Joe: Joe Lee Williams was born in Crawford, Mississippi, in 1903 and died in Macon, Mississippi, in 1982. He hoboed throughout the South, singing, playing guitar, and working outside music. In 1935 he recorded in Chicago and then recorded extensively with a number of artists, including Yank Rachell, Sonny Boy Williamson, Walter Davis, Sonny Terry, and Brownie McGee. Known for his modified nine-string guitar and appreciated for his robust country blues songs, he participated in the folk song revival of the 1960s and 1970s, touring in the United States and Europe. He was active in music into the 1980s.

Williamson, Homesick James: John A. Williamson was born in Somerville, Tennesse, in 1910. He plays bass, guitar, and harmonica. He ran away from home at age ten to perform at dances, taverns, and on the street. He hoboed, playing with Sleepy John Estes, Blind Boy Fuller, and others. In 1930 he moved to Chicago, where he performed and later recorded. He played with John Lee "Sonny Boy" Williamson in the 1940s. He kept playing and recording with many blues artists into the 1980s and now lives in California.

Williamson, Sonny Boy: John Lee Williamson was born in Jackson, Tennesse, in 1914 and died in Chicago, Illinois, in 1948. His unique style changed the harmonica from a novelty instrument into a powerful blues lead instrument. He also parlayed a slight speech impediment into a unique, lazy singing style that became very popular. He traveled and played with Yank Rachell, Big Joe Williams, and Sleepy John Estes, playing with Yank at the Blue Flame Club in Jackson, Tennessee. His first recording was made in 1937, and he recorded with Yank in 1938. He became a key part of the Chicago blues scene, playing clubs and recording with Big Bill Broonzy, Tampa Red, and others. He was so popular that Mississippi blues singer and harmonica player Aleck "Rice" Miller took his name and proclaimed himself the "original Sonny Boy Williamson." In 1948, after leaving a club where he had performed, he was robbed and murdered.

Appendix 5

Brownsville Lynching

The following news item about the Brownsville lynching appeared in the September 1940 issue of *The Crisis* (vol. 47, no. 9), the monthly national publication of the NAACP:

Brownsville Terror

From a river near Brownsville, Tenn., on Sunday, June 23, was fished out the body of Elbert Williams, NAACP leader who had braved the ire of local whites by engaging prominently in the local campaign to get Negroes to vote. Two other NAACP leaders, Rev. Buster Walker, and Elisha Davis were run out of town. Every known pressure had been brought by local whites to discourage Negroes from voting.

Appearing at the Philadelphia NAACP Conference in Tindley Temple in Philadelphia on June 21, Rev. Walker raised $155.47 from the delegates to start a defense fund, after telling his story.

F.D.R. Sent Mob's Names

To President Roosevelt and the Department of Justice the NAACP sent on July 1, the names of the leaders of the mob of sixty whites who drove seven leading

Negroes out of Brownsville, Tenn. Following the "off-the-record" lynching of Elbert Williams.

The names included those of two bank officials, several police officers, a state highway commissioner, and several merchants.

Elisha Davis, one of the refugees, appealed to the country, through the Association, for funds to help his ill wife and seven children. Davis owned and operated a filling station.

Dean William H. Hastie, chairman of the NAACP legal committee, conferred with John O. Rogge, Assistant U.S. Attorney General. Walter White conferred with U.S. Attorny William McClanahan at Memphis, during his investigation of the terrorism.

Officers are posted on all highways leading into Brownsville, turning back all Negroes who do not live there.

F.B.I. Investigates

On July 12, Assistant Attorney General Rogge notified the NAACP: "You will be glad to know that the Federal Bureau of Investigation has been requested to make a thorough investigation of violations of civil liberties of Negroes in Brownsville, Tenn."

Before the resolutions committee of the Democratic National Convention on July 12, appeared a committee of five, headed by NAACP secretary, Walter White, demanding a strong plank on the Negro and describing in detail the Brownsville terror and the "off-the-record" lynching of Elbert Williams.

To the White House on July 19 went another telegram to President Roosevelt protesting the Brownsville terror and asking that immediate steps be taken to wipe it out.

The November issue of *The Crisis* (vol. 47, no. 11) had a follow-up story:

FBI Says It Protected Brownsville Citizens

A letter from the Attorney General's office to the N.A.A.C.P. Stated that Negro citizens of Brownsville, Tenn. who sought to register on September 4 and 5 were protected by Department of Justice agents and did register; but letters received in a roundabout way by the N.A.A.C.P. through third parties all state that no Negroes registered in Brownsville on September 4 and 5.

There is a conflict over what did happen. One letter states that the colored people were afraid to register even though they had been told they would be protected. The terror against Negroes in Brownsville is said to be almost as great as it was during the third week in June when Elbert Williams was lynched for advocating the registration of colored people.

Another item in the same issue of *The Crisis* documented six "officially known" lynchings in Alabama, Georgia, and Tennessee for 1940. Subsequent issues of *The Crisis* didn't have stories on the Brownsville lynching (there were always other lynchings to report) and, as was always the case, no one was prosecuted.

Discography

Sources include Robert M. W. Dixon, John Godrich, and Howard Rye, *Blues and Gospel Records, 1890–1943*, 4th ed. (Oxford: Clarendon, 1997); Mike Leadbitter and Neil Slaven, *Blues Records, 1943–1970*, vol. 1 (London: Record Information Services, 1987); and Mike Leadbitter, Leslie Fancourt, and Paul Pelletier, *Blues Records, 1943–1970*, vol. 2 (London: Record Information Services, 1994); Paul Vernon, *African-American Blues, Rhythm and Blues, Gospel and Zydeco on Film and Video, 1926–1927* (Aldershot, Hampshire, England: Ashgate Publishing Ltd., 1999); and Bengt Olsson, *Memphis Blues* (London: Studio Vista, 1970). This listing includes songs and albums on which Rachell was either the featured performer or an accompanist.

On the pre–World War II 78 rpm recordings the following abbreviations are used for the record labels: Vi for Victor; BB for Bluebird; ARC for American Record Company; Ba for Banner; Cq for Conqueror; Me for Melotone; Or for Oriole; Pe for Perfect; Ro for Romeo; Vo for Vocalion; MW for Montgomery Ward.

Other abbreviations are used to describe the performances: acc. for accompanied by; v for vocal; g for guitar; p for piano; md for mandolin; h for harmonica; vn for violin; sp for speech; wb for washboard; b for bass; and d for drums.

For recordings up to 1941, the number on the left represents the recording master number and take, while the number on the right is the record label's issue number. For later recordings, the LP or CD number and title are given in the session heading and apply to all titles from the session unless otherwise noted. (A different, self-explanatory system is used for the October 16, 1966 session, where the issue details are exceptionally complex.)

There are inconsistencies in the spelling of James Yank Rachell's name, but that is how these titles were released. Before World War II his name was often misspelled "Rachel." When he lived in Tennessee, everyone pronounced it "Rachel," like a woman's name. When he moved up north, more people pronounced it "Ray-shell," consistent with the spelling "Rachell."

RECORDINGS

John Estes
V, acc. own g; Jab Jones, p; Yank Rachell, md.
    Ellis Auditorium, Memphis, TN, Tuesday, September 17, 1929
55531-2   Broken-Hearted, Ragged and Dirty Too   Vi unissued JSP
        CD601 (CD)
uses take 55531-1 and RCA (J) RA5704 (LP) claims to use take 55531-2, but both of these appear to be aurally identical to the issued take of September 26, 1929. The explanation of this anomaly is not known.

John Estes
V, acc. own g; possibly Johnny Hardge or Jab Jones, p; James Rachell, md.
    Ellis Auditorium, Memphis, TN, Tuesday, September 24, 1929
55581-1   The Girl I Love, She Got Long Curly Hair   Vi V38549, BB B7849
The Bluebird reissue may use a different take.

John Estes
V, acc. own g; Jab Jones, p; Yank Rachell, md.
    Ellis Auditorium, Memphis, TN, Thursday, September 26, 1929
55531-3   Broken-Hearted, Ragged and Dirty Too   Vi V38582
55596-2   Divin' Duck Blues   Vi V38549, BB B7677
Take 55531-1 on Victor V38582 appears to be identical to take 55531-3; the explanation of this is not known.

John Estes and James Rachel
James Rachel, v/md; Jab Jones, p; John Estes, g.
    Ellis Auditorium, Memphis, TN, Thursday, September 26, 1929
55597-2   Little Sarah   Vi V38595

John Estes

V, acc. own g; "Tee," h; James Rachell, md.

    Ellis Auditorium, Memphis, TN, Wednesday, October 2, 1929

56335-1   Black Mattie Blues   Vi V38582

John Estes and James Rachell

James Rachell, v/md; John Estes, g; "Tee," h.

    Ellis Auditorium, Memphis, TN, Wednesday, October 2, 1929

56336-2   T-Bone Steak Blues   Vi V38595

Sleepy John Estes claimed that Noah Lewis played harmonica on "Black Mattie." It is not known where the identification of the harmonica player as "Tee" comes from.

John Estes

acc. own g; Jab Jones, p; Yank Rachell, md.

    Ellis Auditorium, Memphis, TN, Thursday, May 13, 1930

59918-2   Milk Cow Blues   Vi V38614, BB B7677

59919-2   Street Car Blues   Vi V38614

John Estes

V-1/James Rachell, v-2; acc. John Estes, g; Jab Jones, p; James Rachell, md.

    Ellis Auditorium, Memphis, TN, Saturday, May 17, 1930

59934-   Expressman Blues-2   Vi 23318

59935-2   Wadie Green Blues-1   Vi unissued

    Ellis Auditorium, Memphis, TN, Wednesday, May 21, 1930

59967-   Whatcha Doin'?-1   Vi V38628

59968-   Poor John Blues-1   Vi V38628

    Ellis Auditorium, Memphis, TN, Friday, May 30, 1930

62547-2   Stack o' Dollars-1   Vi V23397

62548-2   My Black Gal Blues-1   Vi V23397

67549-2   Ninety Pound Mama-1, 2   Vi unissued

67550-   Sweet Mama-1, 2   Vi V23318

Noah Lewis's Jug Band

Noah Lewis, h/v; John Estes, g; Yank Rachell, md; Ham Lewis, j.

    Ellis Auditorium, Memphis, TN, Wednesday, November 26, 1930

64736-2   Ticket Agent Blues   BB B5675

64737-2   New Minglewood Blues   Vi 23266

Previous discographies have listed an unknown mandolinist on "Selling the Jelly," recorded by Noah Lewis's Jug Band on Friday, November 28, 1930, but there is no mandolin present.

Yank Rachel

V, acc. self or Dan Smith, g.
New York City, NY, Monday, February 5, 1934

14776-	Poor James	ARC unissued
14777-	Baby I'm Gone	ARC unissued
14778-	Midnight Snooze	ARC unissued
14779-1	Blue and Worried Woman	Ba 33047, Me M13009, Or 8333, Pe 0278, Ro 5333

All issues of matrix 14779-1 as by *Poor Jim*.

Yank Rachel and Dan Smith

V duet; acc. Yank Rachel, md; Dan Smith, g.
New York City, NY, Monday, February 5, 1934

14780-	Back and Headache Blues	ARC unissued
14781-	Skinny Woman	ARC unissued

Yank Rachel, Charlie Johnson, and Dan Smith

Yank Rachel, v; acc. unknown, p; Dan Smith, g; Charlie Johnson, vn.
New York City, NY, Tuesday, February 6, 1934

14782-	Fare You Well Blues	ARC unissued

Yank Rachel and Dan Smith

Yank Rachel, md; Dan Smith, g; Charlie Johnson, vn.
New York City, NY, Tuesday, February 6, 1934

14787-	Bowlegged Baby	ARC unissued

Matrix 14787 is probably nonvocal, as shown.

Yank Rachell

V, acc. own g; Dan Smith, g.
New York City, NY, Tuesday, February 6, 1934

14788-1	Sugar Farm Blues	Ba 33007, Cq 8355, Me 12958, Or 8319, Pe 0273, Ro 5319
14789-2	Stack o' Dollars	same as above
14790-	Heart of Memphis	ARC unissued
14791-1	Night Latch Blues	Vo 02649
14792-2	Squeaky Work Bench Blues	Ba 33047, Me M13009, Or 8333, Pe 0278, Ro 5333
14793-2	Gravel Road Woman	Vo 02649

Banner 33007 and co-issues as by **Poor Jim with Dan Jackson**; Banner 33047 and co-issues as by **Poor Jim**.

Matrices 14788 to 14792, inclusive, are entered in the ARC files as by **Yank Rachel and Dan Smith**.

Jackson Sheiks
Yank Rachell, md/v; Dan Smith, g/v; Charlie Johnson, vn/v.

New York City, NY, Tuesday, February 6, 1934

14794-	Jab That Thing	ARC unissued
14795-	Gotta Move out of Town	ARC unissued

Yank Rachel and Dan Smith
V duet or solo by one of them; acc unknown, p; probably one of them, g; Charlie Johnson, vn-1.

New York City, NY, Wednesday, February 7, 1934

14796	Blue as I Can Be-1	ARC unissued
14797-1-2	Lonesome Night Blues	ARC unissued
14797-3	Lonesome Night Blues-1	ARC unissued
14798-	Making a Change	ARC unissued
14799-1	Married Man Blues-1	ARC unissued

Dan Smith
V, acc. self or Yank Rachell, g.

New York City, NY, Wednesday, February 7, 1934

14800-	West Alley Blues	ARC unissued
14801-	Brown Gal	ARC unissued
14802-	Eva and Adam	ARC unissued
14803-	Brooklyn Blues	ARC unissued

Walter Davis
V, acc. own p; Yank Rachell, g-1/md-2.

Leland Hotel, Aurora, IL, Sunday, March 13, 1938

020100-1	If You Ever Get Lonesome-1	BB B7663, MW M7505
020101-1	I Did Everything I Could-1	BB B7643
020102-1	When Nights Are Lonesome-1	BB B7589
020103-1	Million Dollar Baby-1	BB B7589
020105-1	If You Only Understand-2	BB B7551, BB B7996, MW M7506
020107-1	Walking the Avenue-1	BB B7512, MW M7507
020108-1	Easy Goin' Mama-1	BB B7551, BB B7996, MW M7508
020109-1	Friendless-1	BB B7663

Matrix 020105 is titled "Pet Cream Blues" on Bluebird B7966, while some copies of Bluebird B7551 are believed to be titled "If You Ever Understood."

Sonny Boy Williamson
V, acc. own h; Yank Rachell, md-1/g-2/possibly sp-4; Joe Williams, g-3/possibly sp-5.
Leland Hotel, Aurora, IL, Sunday, March 13, 1938

020110-1	My Little Cornelius-1, 3	BB B7500, MW M7504
020111-1	Decoration Blues-1, 3	BB B7665, MW M7939
020112-1	You Can Lead Me-1, 3	BB B7536, MW M7765
020113-1	Moonshine-1, 3	BB B7603, MW M7765
020114-1	Miss Louisa Blues-1, 3	BB B7576
020115-1	Sunny Land-1, 3, 4, or 5	BB B7500, MW M7504
020116-1	I'm Tired Trucking My Blues Away-2, 4, or 5	BB B7536
020117-1	Down South-1, 3	BB B7665, MW M7939
020118-1	Beauty Parlor-1, 3	BB B7603, MW M7766
020119-1	Until My Love Come Down-2, 3, 4, or 5	BB B7576, MW M7766

Elijah Jones
V, acc. own g; Sonny Boy Williamson, h-1; Yank Rachell, md/v interjections-2.
Leland Hotel, Aurora, IL, Sunday, March 13, 1938

020120-1	Katy Fly	BB B7616
020121-1	Big Boat	BB B7565
020122-1	Only Boy Child-1	BB B7565
020123-1	Lonesome Man-1	BB B7655
020124-1	Mean-Actin' Mama-1	BB B7616
020125-1	Stuff Stomp-2	BB B7526, MW M7500

Yank Rachell
V, acc. own md-1/g-2; Elijah Jones, g-3/v-4; Sonny Boy Williamson, h.
Leland Hotel, Aurora, IL, Sunday, March 13, 1938

020126-1	J. L. Dairy Blues-2, 3	BB B7525
020127-1	Rachel Blues-2	BB B7523
020128-1	Lake Michigan Blues-1, 3	BB B7602
020129-1	I'm Wild and Crazy as Can Be-2, 4	BB B7602, MW M7498

Walter Davis
V, acc. own p; probably Yank Rachell, g-1/md-2
Leland Hotel, Aurora, IL, Friday, June 17, 1938

020834-1	Angel Child: Part 2-2	BB B7693, MW M7762
020835-1	13 Highway-2	BB B7693, MW M7762
020836-1	Homesick-1	BB B7836, MW M7591

020837-1	If You Treat Me Right-1	BB B7836, MW M7591
020838-1	What Is Wrong with You-2	BB B7792, MW M7763
020839-1	Love Will Kill You-2	BB B792, MW M7763
020840-1	Just Tell Me Your Trouble-2	BB B7745, MW M7764
020841-1	Call Me Anytime-2	BB 7745, MW M7764

Sonny Boy Williamson

V, acc. own h; Walter Davis, p-1; Yank Rachell g-2/md-3/possibly sp-5; Joe Williams, g-4/possibly sp-6.

Leland Hotel, Aurora, IL, Friday, June 17, 1938

020842-1	Honey Bee Blues-1, 2, 4	BB B7707, MW M7940
020843-	My Baby, I've Been Your Slave-1, 3, 4, 5, or 6	BB B7805, MW M7592
020844-1	Whiskey-Headed Blues-3, 4, 5, or 6	BB B7707, MW M7940
020845-1	Lord, Oh Lord Blues-3, 4	BB B7847, MW M7589
020846-	You Give an Account-3, 4	BB B7756, MW M7941
020847-1	Shannon Street Blues-3, 4	BB B7847, MW M7589
020848-1	You've Been Foolin' 'Round Town-3, 4	BB B7756, MW M7941
020849-1	Deep Down in the Ground-2	BB B7805, MW M7592

Yank Rachell

V, acc. own md; probably Joe Williams, g; Sonny Boy Williamson, h.

Leland Hotel, Aurora, IL, Friday, June 17, 1938

020850-1	When You Feel Down and Out	BB B7731
020851-1	Texas Tommy	BB B7731
020852-1	It's All Over	BB B7694
020853-1	My Mind Got Bad	BB B7694

Joe Williams

V, acc. own g; Yank Rachell, md/sp; Sonny Boy Williamson, h-1.

Leland Hotel, Aurora, IL, Friday, June 17, 1938

020854-1	Get Your Head Trimmed Down	BB B7719
020855-1	Peach Orchard Mama-1	BB B7770
020856-1	Haven't Seen No Whiskey-1	BB B7719
020857-1	Goin' up the Mountain	BB B7770

This singer is not Joe Lee "Big Joe" Williams, but another artist, sometimes referred to as "Jackson" Joe Williams.

Yank Rachell

V, acc. own g; Sonny Boy Williamson, h/sp-1/v-2; William Mitchell, bass cano (one-string bass); Washboard Sam, wb; unknown, sp-3.

Chicago, IL, Thursday, April 3, 1941

064104-1	Hobo Blues-1	BB B8768
064105-1	It Seem like a Dream-2	BB B8732
064106-1	Army Man Blues	BB B8840
064107-1	.38 Pistol Blues-1, 3	BB B8732, RCA Vi 20-2955
064108-1	Worried Blues	BB B8840
064109-1	Biscuit-Bakin' Woman	BB B8768
064110-1	Insurance Man Blues	BB B8796
064111-1	Up North Blues (There's a Reason)-1	BB B8796

Yank Rachell

V, acc. own g; Sonny Boy Williamson, h/sp-1; Alfred Elkins, bass cano (one-string bass); Washboard Sam, wb.

Chicago, IL, Thursday, December 11, 1941

070470-1	Yellow Yam Blues	BB B8951
070471-1	Tappin' That Thing	BB B8951, RCA Vi 20-2955
070472-1	Rainy Day Blues	BB B8993
070473-1	Peach Tree Blues	BB B9033
070474-1	She Loves Who She Please	BB B9033
070475-1	Bye-Bye Blues	BB 34-0715
070476-1	Loudella Blues-1	BB B8993
070477-1	Katy Lee Blues	BB 34-0715

Yank Rachell

V/md; Hammie Nixon, h-1/jug-2; Sleepy John Estes, g; Rachell, v/md, v/g only-3.

Chicago, IL, March 6, 1963, Delmark DL-606, Yank Rachell's Tennessee Jug Busters, *Mandolin Blues*. Reissued in 1998 as Delmark DE-606 [CD] with additional tracks as noted.

Texas Tony-1, 2	
Shout, Baby, Shout-1	
Lonesome Blues-1, 3	
I'm Gonna Get up in the Morning-1	
Girl of My Dreams-1	Delmark DE-606
Do the Boogie, Mama, take 3-1	Delmark DE-606
Starvation in My Kitchen-1	Delmark DE-606
Rocky Mountain Blues-1	Delmark DE-606
Do the Boogie, Mama, take 2-1	Delmark DE-606

Chicago, IL, March 31, 1963. This is a second session with the same muscians plus Big Joe Williams, g; and Mike Bloomfield, g.

Up and down the Line-1
Bye-Bye Baby-1
Stop Knockin' on My Door-1
Doorbell Blues
Get Your Morning Exercise-1
When My Baby Comes Back Home-1   Delmark DE-606

Sleepy John Estes and the Tennessee Jug Busters
Estes, v/g; Hammie Nixon, h; Yank Rachell, sp-1/md-2/g-3; Mike Bloomfield, g-4.
   Chicago, IL, March 3, 1964, Delmark DL-608, *Broke and Hungry*. Reissued in 1995 as Delmark DD-608 [CD] with an additional track as noted.

Broke and Hungry-1, 2, 4
Black Mattie-2
3:00 Morning Blues-2, 4
Beale Street Sugar-2, 4
Olie Blues-1, 2
Al Rawls-3   Delmark DD-608
Freedom Loan-2, 4
The Girl I Love-2
Electric Chair-2
Sleepy John's Twist-3

Yank Rachell
V, except 1/sp-1/md-2/g-3; with Mike Bloomfield, p, except 4; John Lee Granderson, g, except 5; Olle Helander, interviewing-1.
   Chicago, IL, Southerland Lounge, May 16, 1964, Jefferson (Sweden) SBACD 12653/4 [CD], *I Blueskvarter: Chicago 1964*, Vol. 1.

Going to Pack up My Things and Go-2
Every Night and Day I Hear My Baby Call
   My Name-2
Texas Tony-1, 2-2   unissued
Texas Tony-3-4   unissued
Bye-Bye Baby-2   unissued
My Baby Rocks Me-2
My Baby's Gone, Soon I'll Be Gone Myself-2
Sometimes I Believe My Baby Treats Me
   Wrong-3, 4   unissued
My Rock Is My Steady Pistol-2, 4, 5   unissued
Interview-1

Recorded by Olle Helander for the Swedish Broadcasting Corporation. A listing of Helander's recordings in the Swedish magazine *Jefferson* lists "My Baby Rocks Me" (which was then unissued) as "Rock Me Baby take 2." Some other titles given by the magazine differ slightly from those later used on the CD.

Yank Rachell

Speech/md; with Shirley Griffith, g.

Indianapolis, IN, June 17, 1964, Flyright (England) LP 523 [LP], *Indianapolis Stomp*.
Indianapolis Stomp

Sleepy John Estes

V/g; Hammie Nixon, h/j-1; Yank Rachell, md.

Newport, RI, July, 25, 1964, Vanguard VRS 9180 [LP], *The Blues at Newport 1964: Part 1*.

        Sleepy John's Twist-1
        Mailman Blues
        Drop Down Mama
        Clean up at Home-1
        Corinna   unissued

Vanguard VSD 77/78 [LP], *Great Bluesmen at Newport*, also issued as VCD 77/78 [CD] includes "Mailman Blues" and "Clean up at Home." Vanguard VCD 115/116 [CD], *Blues Artists at Newport 1959-1964*, includes "Clean up at Home."

Sleepy John Estes

V/g; Yank Rachell, g; Ransom Knowling, b.

Chicago, IL, February 27, 1965, Delmark DL-613, *Brownsville Blues*.
    Government Money

The 1992 Delmark CD *Brownsville Blues* (Delmark DD 613) also includes this track.

Sleepy John Estes and Yank Rachell

V-1/g; with Yank Rachell, v-2/md.

East Berlin, Germany, October, 16, 1966

You Shouldn't Do It-1, 2	Amiga (East Germany) 850.114, 855.114 [LPs]
Tan Little Daddy-1	Scout (West Germany) SC3 [LP]
Yellow Jam Blues-2	Amiga (East Germany) 855.126 [LP] 126

"Tan Little Daddy" and "Yellow Jam Blues" are mistitlings of "Tearin' Little Daddy" and "Yellow Yam Blues," respectively. Amiga 855.114 and Amiga 855.126 are a double LP titled *American Folk Blues Festival '66*. Amiga 850.114 is a single LP, also titled *American Folk Blues Festival '66*. It was reissued on Fontana LPs 855.431TY (West Germany),

681.533TL (France), and STL5389 (England), and on CD as L+R 4.2069 (Germany). Scout SC3 is titled *Up the Country*. "You Shouldn't Do It" is also released on Fono-Ring SFGLP76306 (LP title and country of issue not known). "You Shouldn't Do It" and "Yellow Jam Blues" are reissued on Mojo CD-MOJO-309 [CD], *Blues behind the Wall: East Berlin 1966*.

Sleepy John Estes
V, except 1/g; with Yank Rachell, v-1/g, except 2/md-2.

Hinterbrühl, Austria, October 1966, Wolf (Austria) 120.913 [LP], *1966-1974 Recorded Live*.

   You Don't Mean Me No Good-1
   I've Been Well-Warned [sic]
   Divin' Duck Blues-2
   Interview: Talking and Tuning   unissued
   Clean up at Home-2
   Blues for Johnny
   Mailman Blues
   Three Little Flowers-1
   You Shouldn't Say That

"Three Little Flowers" is mistitled; the lyrics refer to a "pretty little flower."

Sleepy John Estes and Yank Rachel [sic]
Sleepy John Estes, v/acoustic g-1/electric g-2; with Yank Rachell, md.

Vienna, Austria, October 1966, Document (Austria) DLP525 [LP], *Country Blues-Live*.

   I'm a Tearin' Little Daddy-1
   80 Highway-2
   Mailman Blues-1

These recordings are from a TV show.

Yank Rachell
V/md; with Sleepy John Estes, g; Taj Mahal, h-1/g-2.

Chicago, IL, February 12, 1967, Testament TCD 6004, *Mandolin Blues*.

   Dig My Buddy, Joe-2
   Smokey Joe-2
   Rainy Day Blues-1
   My Baby's Gonna Jump and Shout-1

Yank Rachell
V/g, except 1/md-1; Mike Stewart (Backwards Sam Firk) g-1.

Indianapolis, IN, 1973, Blue Goose LP 2010, *Yank Rachell*. Reissued as a CD by Random Chance Records (RCD-2) in 1999.

Tappin' That Thing-1
Pack My Clothes and Go
Skinny Woman Blues
Matchbox Blues
Texas Tony-1
Des Moines, Iowa
Shotgun Blues-1
Sugar Farm Blues
Divin' Duck Blues-1
Wadie Green
Peach Tree Blues

Yank Rachell

V/md; Floyd Jones, electric bass; Pete Crawford, g; Odie Payne, d.

Chicago, IL, August 16, 1979, Delmark LP 649 and cassette tape 649, also CD DD-649,*Chicago Style*.

Depression Blues
Roll Me over Baby
Check up on My Baby
Early in the Morning
Diving Duck
Let Me Tangle in Your Vine
I Don't Believe You Love Me Any More
Going to St. Louis
Sugar Mama

Henry Townsend

V/g-1/p-2; with Yank Rachell, g-1/md-2.

St. Louis, MO, 1979, Nighthawk 201 [LP], *Mule*.

Talkin' Guitar Blues-1
Things Have Changed-2
Dark Clouds Rising-2

Mule has been reissued as Nighthawk HCD 202 [CD].

Yank Rachell

V/md; with Peter Roller, electric g.

Bloomington, IN, 1983, Random Chance Records RCD-1 [CD], *Blues Mandolin Man*.

Wadie Green

Additional track on the 1999 CD reissue of Blind Pig BP 1986 [LP]; for details of the Blind Pig release see session at 1986.

Howard Armstrong

Md; with Yank Rachell, v/md; Ted Bogan, g; "Banjo" Ikey Robinson, banjo; Tom Armstrong, bass.

Chicago, IL, 1985, Arhoolie 1095 [LP], *Louie Bluie*.

.38 Pistol Blues

This film soundtrack LP was reissued in 1998 as Arhoolie CD 470. It also includes two Sleepy John Estes-Yank Rachell tracks from 1929-1930 Victor sessions in Memphis ("The Girl I Love, She Got Long Curly Hair" and "Milk Cow Blues") and "When You Feel Down and Out," Yank Rachell, 1938.

Yank Rachell

V, except 1/speech-1/md; with Peter "Madcat" Ruth, h-2; Peter Roller, acoustic g-2/electric g-3; Sheena Rachell, electric b-3; Leonard Marsh Jr., d-3.

Indianapolis, IN, 1986, Blind Pig BPL-1986 [LP], *Blues Mandolin Man*. Reissued in 1999 as Random Chance RCD-1 [CD], with an extra track, for which see session at 1983.

My Baby's Gone-3
Moonshine Whiskey-3
She Changed the Lock-2
Bugle Call-1, 3
Dreamy-Eyed Woman-3
Cigarette Blues-2
Make My Love Come Down-3
Black Snake-3
Des Moines, Iowa-3

Yank Rachell and Dave Morgan

Yank Rachell, v/md, sp only-1; Dave Morgan, g/except 1.

Indianapolis, IN, November 1994–March 1995, Slippery Noodle Sound SNS0007 [CD], *Pig Trader Blues*.

I Love My Woman
My First Mandolin-1
Slammin' Doors in My Face
Sloppy Drunk
Jump in C
Mistreated Blues
She Caught the Katy
Yank Rachell Boogie
Dark Cloud Rising
I Don't Care How Long You Been Gone

I Can't Go down That Road by Myself
Yellow Yams

John Sebastian

John Sebastian, banjo-1/g-2; Yank Rachell, v/md/sp-3; Jimmy Vivino, electric g-4/ acoustic g-5; Fritz Richmond, j; James Wormworth, washboard/bass d-6/d-7.

Indianapolis, IN, January 25, 1996, Hollywood Records (HR-62227-2) [CD], *Chasin' Gus' Ghost: John Sebastian and the J-Band.*

Yank Rachell Intro-3
Laundromat Blues-1, 4, 6
Tap That Thing-2, 4, 6
My Baby Left Town-1, 5, 7

This was a live performance at a concert in honor of Yank Rachell in Indianapolis; it was organized by his friends and fellow musicians.

John Sebastian

Banjo-1, g-2; Yank Rachell, v/md-3/md-4; Jimmy Vivino, g; Fritz Richmond, j-5/ washtub bass-6.

Indianapolis, IN, 1996, Music Masters 01612-65137-2 [CD], *John Sebastian and the J-Band: I Want My Roots.*

Tappin' That Thing-1, 3, 5
Yank Rachell Boogie-4, 6
Divin' Duck-2, 3, 6

Yank Rachell

V/md; Pat Webb, g; Allen Stratyner, h; Chris Webb, snare d-1/g-2; CJ Watson, g-3; Warren Lacey, electric b-4; Yank Rachell, sp-5; Allen Stratyner-sp-6; Pat Webb-sp-7. Indianapolis, IN, 1997, Flat Rock FRCD-16 [CD], *Too Hot for the Devil.*

Bring It Back Home-1, 3, 4
Too Hot for the Devil-1, 3, 4
.38 Pistol-1, 3, 4
Goin' to St.Louis-1, 4
Decoration Day Intro-5
Decoration Day-1, 4
Worried Blues-1
Pat Webb Blues-1
Yank and Allen Talk about Sleepy John Estes and Hammie Nixon-5, 6
Yank Rachell Boogie-1
Wadie Green-2
Roll Me Over Slow-1
Leave Here Walkin'-1, 4

Potato Diggin' Man-1, 4
Blues for Allen Stratyner-1, 4
Yank Talks about "Sonny Boy" Williamson-5, 6, 7

The following reissue compact disks contain Yank Rachell's vocal recordings made prior to World War II: *James "Yank" Rachel Complete Recorded Works in Chronological Order,* Volume 1 (1934–1938), WBCD-006, and Volume 2 (1938–1941), WBCD-007, these are two CDs produced by Wolf, a blues label in Vienna, Austria, in 1996. *Sleepy John Estes, First Recordings with Yank Rachell and Noah Lewis,* JSP CD 601, is British reissue containing the 1929 Memphis sessions. The Document record label also has issued a CD of these sessions, DOCD-5015.

VIDEOS

Yank Rachell: Tennessee Tornado

This is a 30-minute tribute to Yank produced in 1989 by the Public Broadcasting System affiliate in Indianapolis, Indiana (WFYI-TV). It is distributed by the Center for the Study of Southern Culture at the University of Mississippi. It is also available from Nineteenth Star, a video production company in Indianapolis.

Live at Rosa's

This is a short film shot at Rosa's Lounge in Chicago, Illinois, in 1989. It is directed by Jonathan Letchinger and features the following: Yank Rachell, v-1/electric md; with unknown, electric g-1; unknown, electric b; unknown, d-1.

Early in the Morning-1
Late in the Evening-1
Bugle Call Rag

Louie Bluie

This is a 60-minute documentary about Howard Armstrong, a Tennessee-born string band musician, raconteur, and painter and a friend of Yank Rachell. Yank appears and plays in the film, which was made by Terry Zwigoff.

Selected Song Lyrics

The following are transcripts of a selection of Yank Rachell's recorded songs from 1930 to 1986. The earliest available version of each song is used. During the course of a session there are many interjections from different musicians. Some spoken words and phrases have been included in the transcripts because I think they contribute to the feel of the tune. Sonny Boy Williamson was particulary adept at keeping up a commentary on what Yank Rachell was singing, often prompting a reply from Rachell.

Expressman Blues
Victor 23318, Memphis, Saturday, May, 17, 1930

I said, expressman, expressman, Lord, you have turned your wagon wrong.
Lord, you have turned your wagon wrong.
You took and moved my good girl when I was a long, long way from home.

But a woman make a man do things, and she know darn well that's wrong.
Lord, she know darn well that's wrong.
I just want you to hear poor James singin' these lonesome songs.
(Spoken: Play that thing, boy.)

Baby, if you never, if you never hear me anymore.
Lord, hear me anymore.
Lord, you can 'member one morning, baby, when I walked up on your porch.

Well, I sing this song and ain't goin' to sing no more.
Lord, ain't gonna' sing no more.
I'm gonna put this mandolin under my arm, to the North Memphis Cafe I'll go.

Gravel Road Woman
Vocalion 02649, New York, February 6, 1934

I don't want no skinny mama. I wants a woman, she got a' plenty meat, Lord.
No skinny mama, a woman got plenty meat.
She can rock all night long. Babe, you won't stop to eat.

She won't cook me, cook no breakfast, and she won't wash me no clothes, Lord.
She won't cook me no breakfast. Oooh, she won't wash me no clothes.
(Spoken: What kind of woman is that?)
Well, she won't do nothin' but walk up and down the gravel road.

Baby, it's dark, babe, dark at midnight, and the moon shine down like day, Lord.
Mmmm, dark at midnight, babe, and the moon shine down like day.
I'm gon' find some woman to come and blow all my blues away.

I got up deep, deep in a slumber. I put on my shoes and clothes, Lord.
Ohhhh. I got up in a slumber. Ohhhh. I put on my shoes and clothes.
(Spoken: What you do that for, boy. Play it, Dan.)
I'm gonna try to find my woman. I know she's strolling, babe, on that road.
(Spoken: Play it now.)

Night Latch Blues
Vocalion 02649, New York, February 6, 1934

Well, well, now, baby, you better turn your night lights on.
Eeehee, well, you better turn your night lights on.
And your man may come now knockin', baby, and we sure gonna have some fun.

Well, well, well, well, baby, I know you heard your rooster crow.
Ohhh, baby, I know you heard your rooster crow.
Why don't you throw your man out the window because your husband is knockin' on your door?

Now, now, stay away from my window and stop scratchin' on my screen.
Eeehee, babe, stop that scratchin' on my screen,

Because you're a dirty mistreatment, baby, and I know just what you mean.
(Spoken: Play it, Mister Dan Smith, for Yank Rachell. He gone now. I could die doing this. Crazy man have his fun, cannot stay happy. That's true, boy. That's no jive.)

Well, well, now baby, I know you heard me moan before.
Heeooo. Babe, I know you heard me moan before.
But when your man moans this time, baby, you won't ever hear me moan no more.

Squeaky Work Bench Blues
Banner 33047, New York City, February 6, 1934

Well, I can't love you, baby. I can't love you. I'm a' tell you what's it all about.
I can't love you, baby. I'm goin' to tell you what's it all about.
Babe says, I don't begin to feel worried, honey, until I get in the neighborhood of your house.
Got a old screechy workbench, baby, and your mattress is tore every way.
You have a old screechy workbench, and your mattress is tore every which a'way.
Babe, and you tell me to come and lay down, and I have not got no place to lay.
(Spoken, Yank Rachell: Play it Mister Dan, for me. No baby, I can't use you no more. I'm gonna tell you what's it all about, honey.)

Said, I get my Nunn Bush nasty from walkin' round on your dirty rug.
I get my Nunn Bush nasty from walkin' round on your dirty rug.
Said, I'd rather go by myself, baby, and look to the good Lord up above.

Stack o' Dollars Blues
Banner 33007, New York City, February 6, 1934

Well, well, well, you hear that rumblin', baby, way down in the ground?
Oooo, now, baby, way down in the ground.
And I believe to my soul, must have been my baby jumping down.

I got a stack o' dollars, baby, just as long as I am tall.
Oooooo, now, babe, just as long as I am tall.
Then if you just be my woman, babe, you can have them all.

Now, babe, I send for whiskey, and she brought me gasoline.
Ooooo, now, baby brought me gasoline.
You know, I think I got the meanest woman a poor man most ever seen.
(Spoken: Play it now, boy. Too bad now.)

Sugar Farm Blues
Banner 33047, New York City, February 6, 1934

I said, stop and tell me, baby, where did you get your sugar from?
I said, stop and tell me, baby, where did you get your sugar from?
Baby, well, I believe you got it way down from your daddy's sugar farm.

Ain't but the one thing will give a man the blues.
Ain't but the one thing, oooh, will give a man the blues.
And you haven't got no half-sole, baby, on your last pair of shoes.
(Spoken: Play that thing for me, Mister Dan.)

My baby quit me, and I did not have a chance.
My baby quit me, oooh. I did not have a chance.
And I did not have no back, baby, honey, on my last pair of pants.

J. L. Dairy Blues
Bluebird, B7525, Aurora, IL, March 13, 1938

I got to go, mama. I got to go. I wanna go, now baby, right away.
You know, I got to go. I got to go right straight back home.
You know, I got some milkin' I got to do, mama, way out at the dairy farm.

We got four good milk cows, you know. I have to milk 'em 'bout twice a day.
We got four good milk cows, you know. I have to milk 'em twice a day.
You know, if I don't hurry back home, somebody will be done took all my milk away.
(Spoken: Ah, put 'em on me boy.)

You know, if I don't go and get that milk and butter, somebody sure goin' to carry it away.
You know, if I don't go and get my milk and butter, somebody sure goin' go and carry it away.
And that's how come I'm singin' about the J. L. Dairy. I want to leave this town today.
(Spoken: Hum it out, boy.)

Lake Michigan Blues
Bluebird B7602, Aurora, IL, March 13, 1938

Yes, I went to Lake Michigan, stood on the banks and cried.
Well, I went to Lake Michigan, stood on the banks and cried,
'Cause I want to see my baby over yonder, but it was so long and deep and wide.

And I hung my head, baby, and I slowly walked away.
And I hung my head, baby, and I slowly walked away.
I said, that's all right, Lake Michigan. I hope you'll go dry some day.

Well, the moon got gloomy, Lord. A cloud began to rise.
Well, the moon got gloomy and a cloud begin to rise.
I want to cross Lake Michigan, see my gal on the other side.

And I fell down on my knees, baby, prayed, what shall I do?
Fell down on my knees and I prayed, what shall I do?
Says, I hope some day my baby want to cross Lake Michigan too.

Texas Tommy

Bluebird B7731, Aurora, IL, June 17, 1938

"Texas Tommy" (which is the name of a dance) is the original title, but it
   became "Texas Tony" in Rachell's later recordings.

Texas Tommy, I can ball the jack, indeed, my Lord.
Texas Tommy, I can ball the jack.
I'd do anything, oh Lord, sure thing, to get my woman back.

Mama, mama, know I am your child indeed, oh Lord.
Mama, mama, I know I am your child.
My good work kill me, mama, sure thing. Oh, mama, let me die.

If I could holler, like that streamline, Lord, indeed, my Lord.
If I could holler, like that streamline blow,
I'd holler so loud, oh Lord, sure thing, all on the killing floor.

Shouting, brother, cried the whole night, oh, indeed, my Lord.
Shouting, brother, I cried the whole night long.
I tried so hard, oh Lord, sure thing, to teach him from right from wrong.

Bring my shotgun, pistol, and some shells, indeed, my Lord.
Bring my pistol, shotgun, and some shells.
Me and my woman, oh Lord, sure thing, we going start something here.
(Spoken: Oh, let me go now, boy.)

Texas Tommy, I can ball the jack, indeed, oh Lord.
Texas Tommy, I can ball the jack.
I'd do anything, oh Lord, sure thing, to get that woman back.

Mama, mama, know I am your child, indeed, my Lord.
Mama, mama, I know I am your child.
My good work kill me, mama, oh Lord. Just let this poor boy die.

Hear that rumblin' way down in the ground, indeed, my Lord?
Hear that rumblin' way down in the ground?
Must a' been my woman, oh Lord, sure thing. She sure is jumpin' down.

Army Man Blues
Bluebird B8840, Chicago, April 3, 1941

And I'd rather be a army man, livin' out in Spain.
Be here with these no good women. They doin' everything they can.
I say, yes, mama, mama, I'd rather had be a army man
Than to be here with these no good women, man. These women doin' everything they can.

You know, my mama told me, when I was a boy,
If you join the army, you won't have no more joy.
I told her, yes, mama, mama, I would rather would be a army man
Than to be here with these no good women. You know these women doin' everything they can.

My baby, she told me, I hate to see you go.
If you join the army, I want you to will me your dough.
I told her, no, woman, woman, I will will you my watch and chain
If you just make me a promise, Lord, that you won't give it to no other man.

My dad, he joined the army, when I was a boy.
I said, when I get a man, I want to do the same thing.
I said, yes, daddy, daddy, I wanta be a army man
Than to be here with these no good women, and these women are doing everything they can.
(Spoken: Play it boy. I got 'em now.)

Biscuit-Bakin' Woman
Bluebird B8768, Chicago, April 3, 1941

She bakes her biscuits; she bake 'em just right.
She bakes her biscuits; well, she bake 'em nice.
She's a biscuit-bakin' woman; she's a biscuit-bakin' woman.
I want to tell the world 'bout that biscuit-bakin' woman of mine.

She bakes her biscuits; she bakes 'em nice and keen.
She bakes 'em good enough for the queen.
She's a biscuit-bakin' woman; she's a biscuit-bakin' woman.
I want to tell the world 'bout that biscuit-bakin' woman of mine.

She ain't so tall, but she's kinda low.
She gets her biscuits, 'cause she got good dough.
She's a biscuit-bakin' woman; she's a biscuit-bakin' woman.
I want to tell the world about that biscuit-bakin' woman of mine.
(Spoken: Break 'em down now.)

She bake her biscuits; she don't have to pay no fine.
She's the best biscuit woman in this town.
She's a biscuit-bakin' woman; she's a biscuit-bakin' woman.
I want to tell the world 'bout that biscuit-bakin' woman of mine.

She bakes the biscuits, bake 'em at night.
Wake up in the morning, she got 'em just right.
She's a biscuit-bakin' woman; she's a biscuit-bakin' woman.
She gon' to tell the world 'bout that biscuit-bakin' woman of mine.
(Spoken: Play it now.)

Sing this song before I go.
I want to eat some more of them biscuits that she rolled her dough.
She's a biscuit-bakin' woman; she's a biscuit-bakin' woman.
I want to tell the world 'bout that biscuit-bakin' woman of mine.

Bake this time; ain't gon' bake no more.
If you eat 'em, well, you'll want some more.
She's a biscuit-bakin' woman; she's a biscuit-bakin' woman.
I want to tell the world 'bout that biscuit-bakin' woman of mine.

Hobo Blues
Bluebird B8768, Chicago, April 3, 1941

(Spoken, Yank Rachell: I'm gonna leave my baby this morning.)
Lord, I decided that I would be a hobo. Lord, I hoboed a long, long way from home.
Lord, I decided that I would be a hobo. You know, I hoboed a long, long way from home.
You know, every time I get to thinkin' about my baby, man, I couldn't do nothing but hang my head and moan.

Baby, and every time I decide to hobo, I take the jungle to be my home.
Every time I decide to hobo, Lord, I take the jungle to be my home.
Now you know I'm gonna do just like the prodigal son. I'm goin' back home and acknowledge I done wrong.
(Spoken, Yank Rachell: I ain't going to leave you no more, baby.)

That morning 'bout half past four, Lord, that old freight train begin to reel and rock.
Lord, that morning 'bout half past four, man, that old freight train begin to reel and rock.
(Spoken, Yank Rachell: Lord, have mercy. Sonny Boy Williamson: Oh, honey, hush. Oh, honey, hush.)
You know I went to the door and I looked out. Sonny, I didn't know what it was all about.
(Spoken, Yank Rachell: Now, boy, let's catch it. Take it on down there for me. Washboard Sam, I ain't studyin' you. Mitch, you just whup that can to death.)

Lord, the lightning, it was flashin', boy, the dark cloud risin in the east.
(Spoken, Sonny Boy Williamson: Oh, Yank, let me stay here a little while. Yank Rachell: Yes, my Lord. Listen Sonny.)
Lord the lightning it was flashin', a dark cloud it was risin' in the east.
(Spoken, Yank Rachell: You know, I don't feel good.)
Lord, then I hung my head and I cried, Lord, I wonder what's going to become of me.

Lord, I'm back home with my baby. Lord, I'm just as happy as I can be.
Well, I'm back home with my baby. I'm just as happy as I can be.
But the next time I decide to hobo, I'm going to have my woman right beside me.

Insurance Man Blues
Bluebird B8796, Chicago, April 3, 1941

I just wanted to introduce you to the industrial insurance man.
I just wanted to introduce you to the industrial insurance man.
Well, you know they buried old Turkey Slim; he was electrocuted in the electric chair.

They paid his sister twenty-four hours after the poor boy was dead.
They paid his sister twenty-four hours after the poor boy was dead.
Said, he would pay for anything you die with; you may die in the electric chair.

You may have some kind of accident. Don't be worried be how you die.
You may have some kind of accident. Don't be worried 'bout how you die.
Said, because if you be electrocuted they will pay you anyhow.

Turkey Slim's sister sat down and wrote a letter, back down to the industrial board.
Turkey Slim's sister sat down and wrote a letter, back down to the industrial board.
Say, you done paid me what you promised me, and I don't want you to pay no more.

I'm a old member, and look like I'm going live all the time.
I'm a old member of that company; it look like I'm going to live all the time.
(Spoken, Yank Rachell: I don't want to die.)
Said, but if I should happen to die, Lord, they will that money to my wife.

It Seems like a Dream
Bluebird B8732, Chicago, April 3, 1941

My baby went off, stayed out all night long.
She never got back till the break of dawn.
But it seem like a dream. Well, it seem like a dream.
Well, it seem like a dream. It seem like a dream to me.

I'm gonna buy me a dog, gonna' wire his nose.
Kill somebody 'bout my jelly roll.
Well, it seems like a dream... [etc.]

Me and my baby had a fallin' out.
You didn't know what it was all about.
'Cause it seem like a dream... [etc.]
(Spoken: Play it out, boy. It seem like a dream.)

Now looky here, babe, look what you done done.
Got my money, got me on the bum.
You know, it seem like a dream... [etc.]

Wear my shoes; you wear your sock.
Hear Yank Rachel, how he play that box.
'Cause it seems like a dream... [etc.]

Play this song; ain't goin' play no more.
Puttin' on my shoe; down the street I go.
'Cause it seem like a dream... [etc.]
(Spoken, Play another 'n, boy. I got 'em.)

Tell ya this time; ain't gonna tell you twice.
Don't catch you foolin' around now with my wife.
'Cause, it seem like a dream... [etc.]

Dream that dream all the time.
Don't plain cease, I'm gonna lose my mind.
Well, it seem like a dream...[etc.]

.38 Pistol Blues
Bluebird B8732, Chicago, April 3, 1941

Now run and get my .38 pistol. My woman ridin' around in a V-8 Ford.
Now run and get my .38 pistol. You know my woman riding around in a V-8 Ford.
Well, that must have been my woman gettin' away awhile ago. Oh, there's somebody, Lord, at my back door.

You know I had a little trouble way down 'bout Tom Wilson's place.
You know I had a little trouble way down 'bout Tom Wilson's place.
(Spoken, Sonny Boy Williamson: You better not talk about them people, Yank. They won't let you come back there no more.)
You know it was just on this side of Al Rawls'. It was right down below Mae's place.
(Spoken, Sonny Boy Williamson: Lord, have mercy!)

Now I got a sweet little sweet thing, Sonny Boy, lives down on Lover's Lane.
(Spoken, Sonny Boy Williamson: Oh! What 'cha mean? Tell me what 'cha mean.)
Lord, I got a sweet little thing, and that woman lives down on Lover's Lane.
You know, I'm so crazy about that woman, Lord, I'm scared to call that woman's name.
(Spoken, Sonny Boy Williamson: Yank, let me play one for you. You know I'm gonna do the best I can. Yank Rachell: Do the best you can.)

That's the reason I tote my .38 pistol. That's the reason I carry it every day.
(Spoken: Sonny Boy Williamson: Oh, you must be goin' out bear huntin' or something or other.)
That's the reason I carry my .38 pistol. That's the reason I carry it every day.
(Spoken, Sonny Boy Williamson: I'm glad I didn't meet you when you had it!)
Well, if I catch my baby below Tom Wilson's again, Lord, somebody's sure going to fade away.

Up North Blues (There's a Reason)
Bluebird B8796, Chicago, April 3, 1941

Now I'm going down south. I'm gonna stay until winter's gone.
Now I'm going down south. I'm gonna stay until winter's gone.
Then when the winter gone, then maybe I will go back home.

And I can't stay in the north. You know I ain't got sufficient clothes.
You know I can't live in the north, and I ain't got sufficient clothes.
(Spoken, Sonny Boy Williamson: Oh, Yank, but they sell clothes up there. You know that.)
You know when the wind get to blowin', Sonny Boy, you know I'm even scared to go outdoors.

You know I'm sittin' in the window, and I look out, boy, with tears all in my eyes.
You know I sit in the window, and I look out with tears all in my eyes.
(Spoken, Sonny Boy Williamson: Oh, I know some of your peoples must have died, or something or other, you know.)
You know I want to get outdoors so bad, but, Sonny Boy, you know I'm scared that I would die.
(Spoken: Play it now. Yes, my Lord.)

You know, it's so cold up north the birds they cannot hardly fly.
It's so cold up north the birds they cannot hardly fly.
But every time I step outdoors the wind will cut the water out my eye.

Worried Blues
Bluebird B8840, Chicago, April 3, 1941

The worried blues, mama, they sure do make me feel sad.
Worried blues, mama, sure do make me feel sad.
If the worried blues don't kill me, man, that will be the worst that I ever had.

Now when my baby left me this mornin', it was 'bout half past four.
She said, I don't love you, but still I hate to see you go.
It must have been the worried blues; they sure do make me feel sad.
(Spoken: Lord, have mercy.)
If the worried blues they don't kill me, then, Sonny, that will be the worst I ever had.

You tune in on your radio, call out all ships at sea.
I'm lookin' for Ella Mae, wantin' to know wherever she may be.
The worried blues, they sure do make me feel sad.
If the worried blues they don't kill me, then that will be the worst I ever had.

I can't eat a bite. I can't sleep at night.
If I don't find Ella Mae, you know I'm going to lose my sight.
The worried blues sure do make me feel sad.
If the worried blues they don't kill me, that will be the worst that I ever had.

I said the blues in the morning, first thing when I lay down.
If I don't find Ella Mae I believe I'm gonna lose my mind.
Them worried blues, mama, sure do make me feel sad.
(Spoken: Lord have mercy.)
You know if Yank don't find Ella Mae that will be the worst blues, mama, that I ever had.

Loudella Blues
Bluebird B8993, Chicago, December 11, 1941

Loudella, Loudella, Loudella, don't you hear me callin' you?
Loudella, Loudella, Loudella, don't you hear me callin' you?
Well I wonder why, Loudella, you wanna do me like you do?

Loudella's drinkin' muddy water; now Loudella's sleepin' in a hollow log.
(Spoken, Sonny Boy Williamson: What you mean? You ain't got no house to put her in?)
Loudella's drinkin' muddy water; Loudella's sleepin' in a hollow log.
Loudella have to do the best she can 'cause Loudella's man has gone to the war.

Loudella, I love you. I wonder why that you would run around.
Loudella, I love you, and I wonder why that you run around.
And the way you do me, Loudella, you just drive me 'way from your town.
(Spoken: Oh, play Loudella for me. I want to see her.)

Hate to leave you, Loudella. Loudella, but I got to go.
Hate to leave you Loudella. Loudella, but I got to go.
But when I leave you this time, Loudella, I won't never be back no more.

Hate I love you like I do. Loudella, everybody think you're grand.
Hate I love you like I do, Loudella, and everybody think you're grand.
But just as soon as you get around, Loudella, then someday you will understand.

Peach Tree Blues
Bluebird B9033, Chicago, December 11, 1941

Don't them peaches look mellow hangin' way up in your tree?
Don't them peaches look mellow hangin' way up in your tree?
I like your peaches so well, they have taken effect on me.

I'm gonna get a stepladder, baby. I'm gonna climb up on your top limb.
I'm gonna get a stepladder. I'm gonna climb up on your top limb.

If I get amongst your yellow peaches, you know it's gonna be too bad, Jim. (Spoken: Yes, yes, yes.)

Every time I start to climb your tree, babe, I wonder what make you smile.
Every time I start to climb your tree, babe, I wonder what make you smile.
You wanted me to climb up your tree ever since you was a child.

Tappin' That Thing
Bluebird B8951, Chicago, December 11, 1941

Well, tappin' that thing is easy to do.
I got that thing for my particular use.
I been tappin' thing, great God almighty, been tappin' that thing, great God almighty,
Every morning at eight you can hear me tappin' that thing.

Tap it in the morning; well, I tap it at night.
Tap that thing. I done tap it just right.
Just tappin' that thing, great God almighty, been tappin' that thing, great God almighty.
Every morning at eight you can hear me tappin' that thing.

Went to the front door to get a shine.
Said, go to the back door and get it from behind.
Been tappin' that thing, great God almighty, been tappin' that thing, great God almighty.
Every morning at eight you can hear me tappin' that thing.
(Spoken, Yank Rachell: All right, tap it down, boy.)

Tappin' that thing is easy to do.
I got that thing for my particular use.
Been tappin' that thing, good God almighty, oh, tappin' that thing, great God almighty.
Every morning at eight you can hear me tappin' that thing.

I done told you once; I done told you twice.
Don't be messin' round here with my wife.
You been tappin' that thing, great God almighty, gonna tap that thing.
Every morning at eight you can hear me tappin' that thing.

Wear your shoes; you wear your socks.
You hear Yank Rachell; how he play that box.

He been tappin' that thing, great God almighty, oh, tappin' that thing, great God almighty.
Every morning at eight you can hear me tappin' that thing.
(Spoken, Yank Rachell: Tap it again, boy. I got 'em.)

I don't need no wife. I don't need no hug.
Someone bring me another jug.
I can tappin' that thing, great God almighty, tappin' that thing, great God almighty.
Every morning at eight you can hear me tappin' that thing.

I tap it in the morning, well, I tap it at night.
Tap that thing. I done tapped it right,
'Cause I tap that thing. I been tappin' that thing.
Every morning at eight you can hear me tappin' that thing.
Listen here babe, what you done.
Got my money, got me on the bum.
I been tappin' that thing, great God almighty. I been tappin' that thing, great God almighty.
Every morning at eight you can hear me tappin' that thing.
(Spoken: Oh, tap it now, boy.)

Yellow Yam Blues
Bluebird B8951, Chicago, December 11, 1941

I know you read about me. You know, I'm a stranger in your land.
I know you read about me. Lord, you know, I'm a stranger in your land.
You know I'm that 'tato diggin' man. I just want to tangle up in your potato vine.

I know your 'tatoes need diggin'. Lord, the milk is runnin' out your potato vine.
I know your 'tatos need diggin'. Lord, the milk is runnin' out your potato vine.
That's why I want to dig your potatoes. You know I'm wild about your yellow yams.

You know them yellow yams, them yellow yams, Lord, them yellow yams is restin' on my mind.
(Spoken: Yeah, take them yams on down, boy.)
You know them yellow yams, them yellow yams, them yellow yams is restin' on my mind.
If I catch some man grabbin' my potatoes, Lord, I believe I'll lose my mind.

I said, now come down in my basement. I want you to walk around on my second floor.
Lord, come down in my basement. I want you to walk around on my second floor.

If you want some good diggin' done, have to come down now and knock on my
   door.

Doorbell Blues
Delmark LP 606, *Mandolin Blues*, Chicago, March 31, 1963

Mama, all in my sleep, baby, mama, I can hear my doorbell ring.
Well, all in my sleep, mama, I can hear my doorbell ring.
You know I got up early this mornin', and I could not see a doggone thing.

You know my doorbell is ringin', and my telephone is ringin' too.
Yes, my doorbell's ringin' and my telephone is ringin' too.
That may be my baby, my sweetheart, callin' me. Now what in the world is I gonna do?
(Spoken: Well, all right, all right. Yank Rachell's got the blues.)

My little baby, my little baby, Lord, my baby, she just don't believe in me.
My little baby, my little baby, I swear my little baby, she don't believe in me.
(Spoken: Well, I wonder why.)
She was lookin' for me in Indianapolis on Decatur Street, but I'm goin' home on that
   Katy Fly.

My baby, man, the woman just about to drive me wild.
Whoa, my woman, my little woman, Lord, this gal, she just about to drive me wild.
You know the reason I'm so crazy about my baby, God knows, my baby, she just
   good night huggin' size.
(Spoken: Now play the blues, play the blues. Well, all right.)

Well, well, fare you well, baby. You know I believe I got to go.
Well, fare you well now, fare you well, baby. Yes, I believe now I got to go.
You know, I'm gonna leave here walkin', and I won't be back here no more.

Get Your Morning Exercise
Delmark LP 606, *Mandolin Blues*, Chicago, March 31, 1963

You know, when you want my money, babe, you come and ask me for it.
If I ain't got the money, I'll go somewhere and borrow it.
You just come on in here now, woman, come on and get your mornin' exercise,
'Cause I got a two by four and I'm gonna hew it down to your size.

I get up one the mornin' and I go to work,
But then you put in your call, you go out for a date.
But then, come on in here, baby, come on and get your mornin' exercise,
'Cause I got a two by four, woman. I'm gonna hew it down to my size.

You in the tavern doin' the twist,
Say, looky here, bartender, set up another fifth.
Then, come on in here, baby, and get your mornin' exercise,
'Cause I got a two by four and I'm gonna hew it down to my size.

Way last year they put me in that old rickety jail,
To keep my fists out you women's face.
Just come on in here now, baby. Get your mornin' exercise.
Come on in here and I'm gonna hew you down to my size.

You out all day. I asked you where you been.
Your whiskey tell me you been out with your other man.
Well, just come on in here, baby. Get your mornin' exercise.
I got me a two by four and I'm gonna hew it down to your size.

Matchbox Blues
Blue Goose LP 2010, *Yank Rachell*, Indianapolis, 1973

Hate to see that evenin' sun go down.
And I hate to see that evenin' sun go down.
Well, that makes me think, baby, I'm on my last go 'round.

Settin' here wonderin' would a matchbox hold my clothes.
Said, I'm...
Well, I ain't got so many, baby, but I got so far to go.

Look here, baby, take me back again.
Hey, look here, woman, take me back again.
If you take me back again, mama, I sure will be your good man.

Settin' here wonderin' would a matchbox hold my clothes.
Said, I'm...
Said, I ain't got so many, baby, but I got so far to go.

Sent for whiskey, brought me gasoline.
Said, I sent for whiskey, brought me...
I got the meanest old woman a man most ever seen.

Wadie Green
Blue Goose LP 2010, *Yank Rachell*, Indianapolis, 1973.

You know, I want to see my little old Wadie Green.
Now, I want to see my little old Wadie Green.
You know, I want to see my little old Wadie Green.

Looky here, now, Mary, see what you done done.
Looky here, now, Mary, see what you done.
You make me thought I loved you; now little old Wadie done come.

You know I want to see my little old Wadie Green.
I want to see my little old Wadie...
You know, I want to see my little old Wadie Green.

Little old Mary, she do tolerable well
Little old Mary, she do tolerable...
Lord, but little old Wadie, she is a burnin' hell.
(Spoken: Well, all right, man.)

Cigarette Blues
Blind Pig LP BP1986, *Blues Mandolin Man*, Indianapolis, 1986

My baby, she ain't much more than skin and bones.
People, my baby, she ain't much more than skin and bones.
But, you know, when I get some money, to the hospital my baby goin'.

She laid down last night. I thought she had the flu.
I take her to the doctor and see what he could do.
He said, Yank, I can't help you 'cause your baby dyin' from smokin' cigarettes.
You know, I'm sorry to tell ya, but your baby dyin' from smokin' cigarettes.

I tried to get my baby to stop smokin' cigarettes. She smoke twelve packs a day.
I said, baby, you know that ain't no way to do.
Lord, my baby, my baby dyin' from smokin' cigarettes.
You know I talked to my baby. She said, baby, she said, I'm gonna quit.

I went home the other night. I thought she had the flu.
I take her to the hospital to see what the doctor could do.
You know the doctor told me, I can't do your baby no good.
Well, Yank, I hate to tell you it wadn't no flu and your baby's dyin'.

Bibliography

The following books, articles, and liner notes were used for research about Yank Rachell, his music, associates, and places he lived.

Aarne, Antti, and Stith Thompson. *The Types of the Folktale.* 2nd rev. FF Communications, no. 184. Helsinki: Academia Scientiarum Fennica, 1964.

Baughman, Ernest W. *The Type and Motif Index of the Folktales of England and North America.* Indiana University Folklore Series, no. 20, The Hague: Mouton, 1966.

Buechler, Mark. "Yank Rachell, for Money and Love." *Blues Revue* 29 (June/July 1997): 26–28.

Calt, Stephen. *Yank Rachell.* USA: Blue Goose BG-2010, 1973; USA: Random Chance RCD-2, 1999.

Charters, Samuel. *The Blues Makers.* New York: Da Capo Press, 1991.

Cohn, Lawrence, ed. *Nothing but the Blues: The Music and the Musicians.* New York: Abbeville Press, 1993.

Cook, Bruce. *Listen to the Blues.* New York: Da Capo Press, 1995.

Cushing, Steve, Peter Crawford, and Rich Del Grosso. "James 'Yank' Rachell." *Living Blues* 74 (March/April 1988): 12–21.

Davis, Francis. *The History of the Blues: The Roots, the Music, the People, from Charley Patton to Robert Cray.* New York: Hyperion, 1995.

Del Grosso, Rich. "Styles and Techniques of Great Blues Mandolinists." *Frets* (January 1986): 20–24.

Dixon, Robert M. W., John Godrich, and Howard Rye. *Blues and Gospel Records, 1890–1943.* 4th ed. Oxford: Clarendon, 1997.

Edwards, David "Honeyboy," as told to Janis Martinson and Michael Robert Frank. *The World Don't Owe Me Nothing.* Chicago: Chicago Review Press, 1997.

Garon, Paul A. "Yank Rachell in Louisville." *Blues Unlimited* 6 (November 1963): 3–4. Reprinted in *Nothing but the Blues,* ed. Mike Leadbitter, pp. 259–261. London: Hanover, 1971.

Harris, Sheldon. *Blues Who's Who.* New York: Da Capo Press, 1994.

Haywood County Chamber of Commerce. *Haywood County Historical Guidebook.* Brownsville, TN: Haywood County Chamber of Commerce, 1996.

Herzhaft, Gérard. *Encyclopedia of the Blues.* Fayetteville: University of Arkansas Press, 1992.

James, Michael. "Yank Rachell." *Living Blues* 135 (September/October 1997): 54–55.

Joyce, Mike, and Bob Rusch. "Yank Rachell: An Oral History." *Cadence* 3, no. 1–2 (August 1997): 8, 10, 20.

Koester, Robert. *Yank Rachell and His Tennessee Jug Busters: Mandolin Blues.* USA: Delmark CD DE-606, n.d.; UK: 77 Records 77 LA 12/23, n.d.

Leadbitter, Mike, and Neil Slaven. *Blues Records, 1943–1070.* Vol. 1 (London: Record Information Services, 1987).

Leadbitter, Mike, Leslie Fancourt, and Paul Pelletier. *Blues Records, 1943–1970.* Vol. 2 (London: Record Information Services, 1994).

McCarty, David. "Mandolinist Yank Rachell: Blues for 8 Strings." *Frets* 5, no. 3 (March 1983): 28–30.

Olsson, Bengt. *Memphis Blues.* London: Studio Vista, 1970.

Roller, Peter. "'I Play My Own Style and I Play It on a Mandolin:' Yank Rachell Carrying on an Innovative Blues Tradition." Master's thesis, Indiana University, 1984.

Rowe, Mike. *Chicago Blues: The City and the Music.* New York: Da Capo Press, 1973.

Russell, Tony. "Poor Jim Talks." *Blues World* 11 (November 1966): 5–6.

Santelli, Robert. *The Big Book of Blues.* New York: Penguin Books, 1993.

Sautter, Chris. "Yank Rachell." *Living Blues* 21 (May/June 1975): 45.

Thompson, Stith. *Motif Index of Folk-Literature: A Classification of Narrative Elements in Folktales, Ballads, Myths, Fables, Mediaeval Romances, Exempla, Fabliaux, Jest-Books, and Local Legends.* Vols. 1–6. Bloomington: Indiana University Press, 1955.

Tonneau, Serge. "James 'Yank' Rachell." *Rhythm and Blues Panorama* 42 (1966): 12–13.

Townsend, Henry, with Bill Greensmith. *A Life in the Blues.* Chicago and Urbana: University of Illinois Press, 1999.

Vernon, Paul. *African-American Blues, Rhythm and Blues, Gospel and Zydeco on Film and Video, 1926–1997.* Aldershot, Hampshire, England: Ashgate Publishing Ltd., 1999.

Index

Adams, J. T., 69–70, 78, 87
Alligator Records, 108, 120
"Al Rawls," 32
Alto saxophone, 112
Arkansas, 30, 116
Amsterdam, 75
Armstrong, Howard "Louie Bluie," 118–19
Army Man Blues, 83
Ash Grove Club, 108
Atlanta, Ga., 115
Austria, 75

"Baby Please Don't Go," 36
Baden-Baden, Germany, 75
Banjo, 22, 80
Banjo-mandolin, 110, 111–12
Barbee, John Henry, 36, 37
Bass, 37, 40, 99
Bass horn, 25
Bates, Lefty, 71, 78
Beale Street, 29, 30, 116
Bells, Tenn., 35
Big Hatchie River, 56

Big Road Blues, 116
"Biscuit-Bakin' Woman," x, 48
"Black Mattie Blues," 31
Black Patti, 100
Blackwell, Scrapper (Francis Hillman), 70
Blind Pig Records, 78, 114
Blind Willie's, 115
Bloomfield, Mike, 71, 72, 100, 101
"Blue and Worried Woman," 94
Bluebird Records, 47, 78
Blue Goose Records, 78
Bluegrass music, 94
Blues Brothers, 73
Blues Net Productions, 120
Blues, the: endurance of, 84–86; singing, reasons for, 83–84; style of, 22, 37–38, 71, 73–74, 80–82, 83; teaching of, 78–79, 82; young whites, interest among, 72
Bonds, Son, 36, 117
Bonham, Gordon, 79
Boogie woogie, 36, 65
Boomer's Story, 109
Bootlegging, 23, 40, 44–45

Bottleneck. See Guitar: slide
Boxcar, 27–28, 34
Boyd, Tom, 76
Bracey, Ishman, 90
Bridey, Eric, 25
Brim, John, xv
Brindle, Becki, 78, 79
Broonzy, Big Bill, 49, 50, 117, 118
Brown, Charles, 112
Brownsville Taylor Chapel, 10
Brownsville, Tenn., xv, 9, 22, 24, 27, 28, 29, 30, 37, 39, 41, 43, 45, 49, 56, 57, 62, 63, 69, 79, 94, 104, 109, 139–41
"Bugle Call Rag," 24
Butterfield, Paul, 72

California, 36, 65, 72, 73, 99, 113
Calloway, Cab, 42
Cannon, Gus, 33, 112
Carr, Leroy, 71
Charles, Ray, 112
Charters, Sam, 109
Chatman family, 91
Chicago Blues Festival, 120
Chicago, Ill., x, 26, 38, 39, 41, 43, 46, 49, 50, 57, 66, 68, 71, 72, 96, 99, 102, 103, 105, 107, 116
Chicago Style, 72, 80, 81
Church, 12–13, 41
Clark, Huey, 32
Clarksdale, Miss., 116
Cleveland, Ohio, 65
Cooder, Ry, xvii, 108–14
Copenhagen, 75
Cotton, 5, 7, 8, 10, 14, 74
Covington, Tenn., 44
Country suppers. See House parties
Crawford, Pete, 72
Crawfordsville, Ind., 122
Crisis, The, 139–41
Crosstune, 22
Czechoslovakia, 75

Davenport, Iowa, 120
Davis, Jim, 25
Davis, Miles, 100
Davis, Walter, 46, 94, 97

Dayton, Tenn., 118
Decca Records, 100
"Deep Down in the Ground," 95
Deer Creek Music Center, 120
DelGrosso, Rich, 89–91
Delmark Records, 71, 72, 77, 99
DeMyer, Larry, xvii, 78, 79, 83, 85
Des Moines, Iowa, 96
Detroit, Mich., 41, 57
Devil's Son-in-Law. See Wheatstraw, Peetie
"Divin' Duck Blues," 31, 83, 98, 118
"Doorbell Blues," 71
"Down South Blues," 47
Drinking, 34, 35, 39, 44, 46, 50, 64, 66, 67, 71, 102, 104
Dyersburg, Tenn., 36

Earl McDonald's Louisville Jug Band, 110, 112
Edwards, David "Honeyboy," xv, 116–18
England, 75
Estes, Sleepy John, x, xvi, xvii, 7, 22, 23, 24, 25, 29, 30, 31, 32, 33, 34, 35, 37, 38, 39, 40, 42, 43, 47, 49, 57, 58, 64, 66, 68, 71, 72, 73, 77, 84, 87, 89, 90, 96, 99, 101, 102, 103, 104, 107, 108, 109, 110, 111, 112–13, 114, 117, 118
European tours, 71, 75–78
Evans, David, 93–96, 116
Even Dozen Jug Band, 101
Exchange and Front Street, 30
"Expressman Blues," 31

FBI, 140
Fickle Pickle, 103
Fiddle. See Violin
Florida, 115
Franklin, Pete, 70–71
Franklin, Stoke, 37
Franklin, Walter, 37
"Freedom Bank," 32
Fuller, Jesse, 103

Gandy, Pie, 25
Garvin Gate Blues Festival, 120
Gary, Tommy, 87
Geneva, 75
Germany, 75, 77

"Get Your Morning Exercise," 71
Ghosts, 14
Gibson, 110, 113
"Girl I Love, She Got Long Curly Hair, The" 109
"Goin' to Brownsville," 83
"Goin' to Brownsville, taking the right-hand road...," 109
Gospel music, xv, 40–41, 83
Gospel String Band, 41
Goss, Son, 37
"Government Money," 96
Grafeyphone, 21
"Gravel Road Woman," x
Griffith, Shirley, 69–71, 78, 87
Guitar, 20, 21, 22, 23, 24, 25, 36, 37, 38, 39, 49, 50, 57, 58; nine-string, 36; boogie woogie, 65–66, 70, 72, 77, 78, 80, 81, 90; slide, 49, 111, 118
Guy, Buddy, 120

Haints, 14, 55
Harlem Hamfats, 91
Harmonica, 22, 38, 39, 40, 42, 43, 72, 80, 117
Harp. *See* Harmonica
Hatcher, Willlie, 91, 105
Hayley, Sharron, 37
Haywood County, 45
"He went down to Clifton, get some alcohol...," 71
"Hey, Black Mattie, where you sleep tonight?...," 31
High Sheriff from Hell. *See* Wheatstraw, Peetie
"Highway 61," 66
"Hobo Blues," x
Hoboing, 34
Holland, 75
Holland Tunnel, 107
Hooker, John Lee, xvi
Horton, Shakey (Walter Horton), 107
House Parties, 23–24, 33, 34, 42, 70, 107
House, Son (Eddie House), 103
Howell, Peg Leg (Joshua Barnes Howell), 90
Howlin' Wolf (Chester Burnett), 104
Humboldt, Tenn., 35, 39
Hurt, Mississippi John, 108

"If the ocean was whiskey and I was a divin' duck...," 119
Iglauer, Bruce, 120
"I got a stack o' dollars as long as I am tall...," 31
"I got four cows to milk...," 44
"I'm gonna get my .38 pistol...," 47
"I'm Tired Trucking My Blues Away," 94
Indian, 6
Indiana, 119
Indiana Blues Society, 119; Yank Rachell Birthday Bash, 120
Indianapolis, xv, xvi, 13, 40, 41, 44, 65, 68–71, 72, 79, 82, 83, 98, 103, 109, 117, 120, 121, 122
Indiana University, 114
"Insurance Man Blues," 48
"I wannna to see my little old Wadie Green...," 48

Jackson, Jim, 37
Jackson, Miss., 70
Jackson Shieks, 93
Jackson, Tenn., 37, 38, 39, 41, 42, 43, 68
James, Skip (Nathaniel James), 103
Jazz, 84–85, 91, 96
Jazz Record Mart, 99, 100, 104
Jefferson, Lemon (Blind Lemon), 21, 95
"J. L. Dairy Blues," 44
J. L. Dairy farm, 58
"John Henry was a steel driving man...," 37
Johnson, B., 37
Johnson, Blind Willie, 111
Johnson, Doris, 119–22
Johnson, Lonnie, 112, 117, 118
Johnson, Robert, 112
Johnson, Stormy, 79
Johnson, Wardell, 41
Jones, Jab, 29, 30, 31, 109, 110, 112
Jug, 29, 33, 72, 101, 117
Jug bands, 29, 33, 108, 112, 114

Keil, Charles, 116
Kentucky, 110
Kid Spoon, 63
King, B. B., xv, xvi, 73, 76, 80, 82, 118
King, Eric, 115

King, Tom, 59, 60–61
KKK (Ku Klux Klan), 57
Koester, Bob, 71, 72, 99–103, 104
Kosciusko, Miss., 103
Kweskin, Jim, 101

"Lake Michigan Blues," x, 47
"Lawyer Clark," 32
Legend of Sleepy John Estes, The, 99
Lewis, Furry (Walter Lewis), 90
Lewis, Ham, 33
Lewis, Noah, 30
Life in the Blues, A, 97
Lippman, Horst, 75
Little Walter (Marion Walter Jacobs), 39
Lockwood, Robert, Jr., 65
Lomax, Alan, 103, 116
"Lonesome Blues," 71
Louie Bluie, 118
Louisville, Ky., 120
Lynching, 56–57, 139–41

Mae's place, 47–48
Mandolin, ix, xvi, xvii, 17, 18, 19, 20, 21, 22, 25, 37, 38, 40, 41, 50, 73, 77, 79; electric, 80–81
Mandolin Blues, 99, 101
Martin, Carl, 95
"Matchbox Blues," 94, 96
McCoy, Charlie, 91, 95, 102
McDowell, Fred, 103
Melrose, Lester, 43, 46, 47, 48, 49
Memphis, Tenn., x, xvi, 27, 29, 30, 33, 35, 49, 79, 80, 106, 107, 108
Memphis Jug Band, 116
Memphis Minnie, 35, 36
Milan, Tenn., 35
Milwaukee, Wis., 114, 115
Mississippi, 64, 116
Mississippi Delta, x
Mississippi Hot Footers, 91
Mississippi Mud Steppers, 91
Mississippi Valley Blues Festival, 120
Missouri, 63
Moman, Johnny, 107
Montgomery, Little Brother (Eurreal Wilford Montgomery), 75, 100

Montgomery, Wes, 84
Moonshine (whiskey), 7
Moore, John, 44
Morgan, Dave, 79, 122–23
Mother Blues, 104
"Move Your Hand," 71
"Move your hand off that rusty can...," 71
Musselwhite, Charlie, xvii, 72
Muddy Waters (McKinley Morganfield), 39, 73, 103, 104
Mud Island, 106
Mule, 98
"My baby caught the Katie, left me a mule to ride...," 73

NAACP, 139–40
Nashville, Tenn., 37
Newbern, Hambone Willie, 21, 22, 37
Newport Festival, 72, 102
New York, xvi, 29, 41, 42, 57, 79, 107
Nighthawk Record Company, 98
Nighthawk, Robert (Robert McCoy), 103
Nixon, Hammie, 33, 36, 38, 39, 40, 42, 72, 77, 87, 99, 101, 103, 106, 109, 117, 118
Nobelsville, Ind., 120
North Pole, 75
Norway, 75
Nutbush, Tenn., 40

"Pack My Clothes and Go," 94
Paducah, Ky., 34
Paramount, 100
Paris, France, 75
Paris, Tenn., 27
Peabody Hotel, 80
"Peach Tree Blues," x, 47, 48, 96
Pearl Harbor, bombing of, 63
Peer, Ralph, 29
Peete, Peter, 104
Philadelphia, Pa., 139
Piano, 64, 72, 73, 94, 95, 111
Pickett, Charlie, 66, 94
Pig Trader Blues, 122
"Pig Trader Blues," 79
Plugged Nickel, 100
Police, 23, 30, 45, 50, 63

Index

Rachell, A. B. (brother), 6
Rachell, Ella Mae (wife), 37, 40, 69
Rachell, George (father), 5–6, 8, 9, 18
Rachell, James, Jr. "Big J. C." (son), xv, 40
Rachell, James "Yank": baptism of, 13; education of, 10–11; guitar style of, 93–96, 98, 103, 105, 111, 114, 117, 118; individual musical expression, 115; mandolin, style and tuning of, 89–91, 94, 95, 98, 102, 105, 110, 111, 113, 114, 115, 116, 117, 118; married, to Ella Mae, 40; pig, trading for a mandolin, 17–20; on sharecropping, 3–5; on songwriting, 31, 47
Rachell, Jess (son), 40
Rachell, Leslie (brother), 6–7
Rachell, Lula (mother), 9, 17–19, 23, 25
Rachell, Maenell (daughter), 40, 69, 83
Rachell, Sheena (granddaughter), 40, 65, 83, 99, 115
Rachell, Tracy (granddaughter), 40, 83
Rachell, Willa B. (daughter), 10, 40, 83
Railroad, 25, 26, 27–29
"Rainy Day Blues," 95
Rap, 84–85
Rawls, Al, 32, 47
Rawls, Augie, 17, 19
Rawls, Jess, 37
Recordings: with Dan Smith, 41–42; with Dave Morgan, 79; for Delmark, 71; with Henry Townsend, 64–65; with John Sebastian, 79; with Sleepy John Estes and Jab Jones, 29–31; with Sonny Boy Williamson, 42, 43, 46–49; with Pat Webb and Allen Stratyner, 81
Red Beans and Rice, 79
Ripley, Tenn., 30, 36
Rock and roll, 81–82, 84
Roller, Peter, 114–16
Roosevelt, President Franklin D., 139
Royalties, 30–31, 47, 69, 72, 73, 77–78
Rush, Otis, 73, 77
Russia, 75

Santa Monica, Calif., 113
Sebastian, John, 79, 80, 83, 120
"Send for whiskey . . . ," 21
Shade, Will, 33, 107

Shaw, Jimmy Joe, 117
Shaw, Miss., 116
"She Caught the Katie," 69
Shelby, Miss., 97
"Skin and Bones," 47
"Skinny Mama," 105
Sleepy John. *See* Estes, Sleepy John
Slippery Noodle, 72, 78, 107
Slippery Noodle Sound, 122
Smith, Bessie, 21
Smith, Clydell, 107
Smith, Don, 41, 42
"So cold up north, the bird can't hardly fly . . . ," 76
Somerville, Tenn., 107
Son Brimmer. *See* Shade, Will
Sonny Boy. *See* Williamson, John Lee "Sonny Boy"
Spanish (tuning), 118
Spann, Otis, 73
Spivey, Victoria, 101
"Stack o' Dollars," x, 31, 94, 95
Stevens, Bob, 22
St. Louis Jazz Heritage Festival, 121
St. Louis Jimmy (James Burke Oden), 66
St. Louis, Mo., 46, 59, 60, 62–66, 95, 97, 98, 117
"Stop Knockin' on My Door," 72
Stratyner, Allen, 81
String bands, 94, 118
"Sugar Farm Blues," x
Sunnyland, Slim (Albert Luandrew), 66, 75
Swaggie Records, 110
Sweden, 75
Switzerland, 75
Sykes, Roosevelt, 95

Taj Mahal (Henry Saint Claire Fredricks), 69, 73
Tampa Red (Hudson Whittaker), 49, 117
"Tappin' That Thing," x, 83
Taylor, Bud (Daniel) (uncle), 20
Taylor, Henry (cousin), 20
Taylor, Horace (grandfather), 9, 10
Taylor, Rose (grandmother), 9, 10
Tennessee, 107, 110
Tennessee style, 117

"Texas Tony," 37
".38 Pistol Blues," x, 47, 48, 73, 83
Thornton, Robert, 44, 60–61
Three Js jug band, 29, 33, 93
Tom Wilson's Place, 47–48
Too Hot for the Devil, 81
Tornado Jug Band, 33
Townsend, Henry, 36, 64–65, 95, 97–99, 120
Trenton, Tenn., 35
Trombone, 25
Tuba, 112
"Turkey in the Straw," 24
"Turkey Slim, he died in the electric chair...," 48
Turner, Tina, 40

"Up North Blues," x, 47
Urban Blues, 116

Vanguard Records, 103
Van Ronk, Dave, 101
Vastapol (tuning), 118
Victor Records, xvi
Violin, 25, 37, 38, 93, 114, 117
Vocalion, 100

"Wadie Green," 48, 94
Walker, Jimmy, xv, 66, 72
Walker, T-Bone (Aaron Walker), 96
Wallace, Sippie (Beulah Wallace), 75
Washboard, 23
W. C. Handy festival (Awards), 58, 79, 106
Webb, Pat, 79, 81, 85
Welding, Pete, 101
Wells, Junior, 75, 77
"Well, you may be sweet...," 37

West African music, 114
West Hollywood, Calif., 108
West Tennessee, x, 107
WFYI, xvi
Wheatstraw, Peetie, 64, 95
Whiskey, 32, 39, 42, 43, 45, 46–47, 72
White, Bukka (Booker White), 103
White people, 9–10, 24, 26, 56–62, 84, 85–86, 122–23
White whiskey, 23, 24, 35, 41, 50, 51
Williams, Big Joe, 36, 46, 71, 72, 87, 98, 99, 100, 101, 104, 117
Williams, Elbert (Albert) "Big Williams," 56, 139–41
Williams, Mayo, 100
Williamson, Homesick James (John A. Williamson), 36, 65, 103, 104, 107
Williamson, John Lee "Sonny Boy," x, 7, 34, 41, 42, 43, 44, 46, 47, 50, 66–68, 87, 94, 95, 98, 105, 107; death of, 67–68
Wilson, Tom, 47
Wisconsin, 114
Wisconsin Conservatory of Music, 115
Wolf Trap, 118
"Wonder would a matchbox hold my clothes?...," 21
World Don't Owe Me Nothing, The, 116
"Worried Blues," 49
"Worried blues sure make a man feel bad..., The," 49

"Yellow Yam Blues," x, 47
"You Are My Sunshine," 24
Young, Johnny, 102, 103

Zochowski, Jay, xvi
Zwigoff, Terry, 118, 119

www.ingramcontent.com/pod-product-compliance
Lightning Source LLC
Chambersburg PA
CBHW030344240426
43661CB00052B/1735